PENGUIN BOOKS

Rx FOR READING

Barbara J. Fox has a Ph.D. from the University of North Carolina
and is an Associate Professor of Graduate Studies in Reading at
North Carolina State University. The author of *Teach Your Child
to Read in Twenty Minutes a Day,* Fox is particularly interested in
elementary-school reading programs and has been a second-
grade teacher. She lives in Chapel Hill, North Carolina, with her
husband and their two elementary-school-aged children.

Rx FOR READING

HOW THE SCHOOLS TEACH YOUR CHILD TO READ AND HOW YOU CAN HELP

BARBARA J. FOX, PH.D.

PENGUIN BOOKS

PENGUIN BOOKS
Published by the Penguin Group
Viking Penguin, a division of Penguin Books USA Inc.,
40 West 23rd Street, New York, New York 10010, U.S.A.
Penguin Books Ltd, 27 Wrights Lane,
London W8 5TZ, England
Penguin Books Australia Ltd, Ringwood,
Victoria, Australia
Penguin Books Canada Ltd, 2801 John Street,
Markham, Ontario, Canada L3R 1B4
Penguin Books (N.Z.) Ltd, 182–190 Wairau Road,
Auckland 10, New Zealand

Penguin Books Ltd, Registered Offices:
Harmondsworth, Middlesex, England

First published in Penguin Books 1989

1 3 5 7 9 10 8 6 4 2

LIBRARY OF CONGRESS CATALOGING IN PUBLICATION DATA
Fox, Barbara J.
Rx for reading: how the schools teach your child to read and how you
can help/by Barbara J. Fox.
p.   cm.
Bibliography: p.
1. Children—Books and reading.   2. Reading—Parent participation.
I. Title
Z1037.A1F69   1989
028.5′3—dc19   88-37323
ISBN 0 14 01.0703 7

Printed in the United States of America
Set in Baskerville
Designed by Ann Gold
Illustrations by Donald L. Fox

To my parents, Jeanne and Edward, who were my first teachers. And to my children, Susan and Brian, with whom I have shared so many wonderful children's books.

My special thanks go to Don, my husband, for his support and encouragement during the many hours I spent writing this book. The drawings of the learning activities are his special contribution to the completed manuscript.

CONTENTS

RX FOR READING

1

READING INCENTIVES

"I just read the greatest book!" "Mom, can't I stay up just twenty more minutes so I can finish this chapter?" "Dad, will you read one more book before I go to bed? Please?" This is how we want our children to feel about reading— enthusiastic, energized, excited about books.

Toddlers who sit happily on their parents' laps and point to illustrations in picture books learn that books are an important part of everyday experiences. Preschoolers who look forward to Mom and Dad reading storybooks at bedtime are well on their way to becoming avid readers. Elementary school children who routinely read for pleasure will continue to do so as adults.

Of the thirteen years it will take your child to move from kindergarten to his senior year in high school, the first seven are the most important. In the elementary grades, beginning with kindergarten and ending with sixth grade, your child learns every essential ability necessary to become a literate, highly skilled adult reader. Without question, learning the reading abilities taught at each grade and spending leisure time reading books are crucial for becoming a skilled reader.

THE HOME-SCHOOL CONNECTION

If your child is in the elementary grades or about to enter kindergarten, now is the time to make a special effort to help with reading. Your child is more likely to welcome your help now than at any other time in his schooling. It is equally important to note that the school puts the most time and energy into teaching reading when your child is in the elementary grades.

Giving your child the guidance and support necessary to do well in school today is not an option—it is a necessity. It's not how much money you make, the cost of your house, or where you go on vacation—what translates into success in school is giving your child help when he needs it and working together with the school to place a high value on reading for pleasure.

This is where prescriptions for reading come in. Effective prescriptions for reading are like other well-thought-out remedies—a combination of doing the right thing the right way. For reading, this means realizing what abilities your child needs to practice, and coordinating your home-based activities with the abilities your child is learning in school.

Your child's school is willing and eager to make the home-school connection work; teachers and principals know they cannot successfully educate your child without your assistance. Knowing how to help your child and how to work cooperatively with the teacher is what this book is all about. You'll learn how the elementary school reading program works, how to find and share books that match your child's reading ability, how to talk successfully with the teacher, what reading test scores mean, how to recognize the early signs of reading difficulty, and how to help your child with phonics, vocabulary, and comprehension at home.

READING SPARK PLUGS

In order to make the most of what the school reading program has to offer, your child needs a lot of reading practice. Some children are born readers—they always have a book nearby and their enthusiasm for reading lasts a lifetime. Other children, who can be equally good readers, need an extra special spark to ignite their interest in books.

Spark plugs are incentives to get going, to generate interest in books, to become convinced that being a good reader is important. Reading spark plugs are for the child who, for whatever reason, has a lackluster interest in books. If your child doesn't spend any leisure time reading, or reads very little, reading spark plugs are the right prescription.

When your child reads a book, it is generally for one of two reasons—a love of reading, or a special incentive. If your child's motivation comes from within, the personal satisfaction that comes from reading is reward enough. Children like this, who are internally motivated, need no reading spark plugs.

But what is the source of internal motivation? It comes from having pleasurable experiences with books. One good experience builds on another until reading is a positive and integral part of your child's life. Sharing your child's experiences with books is a wonderful way to help him appreciate good literature. You'll find ways to do this in Chapter 3, Sharing Books with Children.

What happens if your child doesn't get the message that reading is a worthwhile leisure pastime? What should you do when the teacher sends something home for your child to read, and you know it's important to follow through, but your child's enthusiasm is lagging? How can you give your child sufficient reading opportunities so that he learns firsthand the importance of reading and the pleasure of finding a good book?

It is somewhat like starting your car on a cold winter morning. Occasionally the engine takes a few cranks to get going. It's not that there's anything amiss with the engine; it's just that in exceptionally cold weather engines have more difficulty starting. Just like your car on a cold morning, every now and then children take an extra boost to get started reading. That's where reading spark plugs come in.

Having been a reading specialist in classrooms and remedial reading clinics—including the reading clinic at the university where I teach—I have come to realize that some of the simplest ideas are often the most motivating. Following this line of reasoning, I would like to share six tried-and-true, simple, effective methods for turning hesitant readers into avid readers.

Use the ideas you believe your child will find most appealing and modify them as you wish. But remember, for spark plugs to work, your child must value the reward he sees for his efforts. Once your child becomes accustomed to reading, he'll come to appreciate books and will read because he wants to, not because he's anticipating something in return.

Use cooperative reading. On evenings when Courtney does a lot of foot-dragging about reading the books her second-grade teacher sends home, Courtney's mother uses a superb reading incentive.

Sitting down beside Courtney her mother says, "You know, I've been thinking it would be fun to take turns reading. First I'll read half a page out loud while you follow along with your eyes. When I'm done, I'll close the book and ask you a question. Then it's your turn. You read half a page and ask me a question. Ready? I'll go first."

This simple activity appeals to children of all ages, requires absolutely *no* preparation, and does wonders to improve comprehension.

Originally used to help children ask good questions and focus on meaning (57),* this reading incentive captivates even the most reluctant reader. Several years ago we were faced with a real challenge when a fifth-grader came to the university reading clinic. After four and a half years of failing in school, Preston refused to read. Even though we tried all sorts of inducements, Preston wouldn't use the few reading abilities he had. Nothing worked until we tried the easy activity I just described.

Children like Preston refuse to read because they are afraid of failure. Children like Courtney, who are occasionally reluctant to pick up a book, are experiencing the normal ups and downs in enthusiasm that go along with learning to read. Still other children balk at reading because they think it will take too much time and effort.

Whatever the reasons for their reluctance, this activity provides children with a reading companion. Reading with someone else seems less burdensome and, perhaps as important, offers the challenge of trying to stump the other reader with a good question.

Dividing long passages into smaller, bite-sized pieces makes reading more manageable. There is no hard and fast rule for how much should be read at once—any workable length is fine. Courtney's mother divided pages in half; Preston, because he was an unusually poor reader, began by reading one sentence at a time. As a rule of thumb, start out as Courtney's mother did. Ask your child to read more if half a page seems too easy, less if half a page seems cumbersome.

*The numbers in parentheses throughout refer to the Notes section at the end of the book.

Give comic books a try. Comic books, while a bit out of the mainstream, are a great way of opening the door that leads to a more serious interest in books. Many fourth-, fifth-, and sixth-graders find comic books spellbinding, yet resist reading books. Granted, comic books are not high-quality literature. Neither you nor I would want our children fed a steady diet of comic books for any length of time. Still, comic books ought not to be overlooked since they provide your child with much-needed reading practice.

If your child comes home from school and immediately plants himself in front of the television, you need a powerful reading incentive, one that offers the same imagery that television does. To a large extent, comic books have this quality. Think of them as a bridge between your child's current lack of interest in books and future commitment to leisure reading.

Whenever I prescribe comic books as a reading spark plug, I recall Marcus, a fourth-grader who was absolutely impossible when it came to leisure reading. His mother and I tried all sorts of incentives, but our efforts were futile. Then Marcus's father brought a comic book home from a business trip. Marcus wasn't interested initially, but the color and illustrations were too enticing to resist for long, and he was soon absorbed in comics.

Instead of watching television every spare minute, Marcus spent some of his free time reading. Having picked up the habit of using leisure time for reading, it wasn't such a big step for Marcus to branch out to books. His mother got him interested in an adventure series, which was all it took to convince Marcus that reading was a great way to spend free time.

Introduce your child to a captivating series of books. As a reading spark plug, getting your child interested in a series of books is as effective as they come. You probably remember reading *Nancy Drew* and the *Hardy Boys* from your own childhood. Most of the series you'll recall from your school days are still in the public library, along with some wonderful new collections.

My daughter, Susan, likes the detective stories featuring Nate the Great, written by Marjorie Weinman Sharmat (1). The books in this series, which are just right for children who read on a first- or second-grade level, follow Nate the Great as he solves baffling cases. Mysteries are great fun for children of all ages, and this series is written with a nice touch of humor.

The best way to discover a series is by asking the librarian in the youth section of your public library for suggestions. To give you a start, I'd like to share some long-standing favorites. For younger children, say first-graders, the *Amelia Bedelia* books, written by Peggy Parish (2), are terrific. This series is about the humorous episodes that arise when Amelia Bedelia, a maid for the Rogers family, interprets even the most common phrases literally—phrases like "pitch a tent" or "prune the bushes."

Another excellent series for young readers is Arnold Lobel's *Frog and Toad* books (3). Forest creatures with humanlike qualities, Frog and Toad go from one adventure to the next, helping each other out of all sorts of predicaments. Look for these series on shelves labeled "Easy Readers" in your public library.

If your child is in second, third, or fourth grade, try the *Encyclopedia Brown* series. Written by Donald Sobol (4), each book in this unique series features several short, bite-sized mysteries that can be finished in a single sitting. The mysteries feature Encyclopedia Brown, a young boy with a good eye for solving perplexing cases. Each mystery is one chapter long and ends with a question asking your child to solve the case. Encyclopedia Brown's solution is given at the end of the book. The idea that your child can read one whole mystery in a short time is a real motivator.

Mature second-grade readers, and children in grades three through six, enjoy the *Great Brain* books by John D. Fitzgerald (5), a series based on the outlandish adventures of a boy living in a small town at the turn of the century. And Beverly Cleary (6) has written wonderful books for advanced second-grade readers, and third- through fifth-grade children. Look for Cleary's books about Henry Huggins and about Ramona. Your child will identify easily with Cleary's down-to-earth characters and with her sensitive, humorous portrayal of personalities and family life.

Other favorite series of children in grades four through six are the *Black Stallion* by Walter Farley (7) and the series of horse stories by Marguerite Henry (8). Be sure to look also for the series of stories featuring Lynn, a likable girl who has intriguing adventures, written by Phyllis Reynolds Naylor (9). Among the most sophisticated series are *The Prydain Chronicles* by Lloyd Alexander (10), *The Dark Is Rising* by Susan Cooper (11), and a three-part series beginning with *A Wrinkle in Time* by Madeleine L'Engle (12). Written for fifth-, sixth-, and seventh-graders, these three series tell of quests and brave children, and of intriguing adventures in time and space, using intricate plots involving menacing forces. As other children have, your child will surely get caught up in the spellbinding fantasy woven by these authors—one of the most effective reading spark plugs.

When you go to the library, check out one book each from several series and ask your child to try each book. The one your child finds most intriguing is the series you want to follow up on. Once your child has become interested in one book in a series, the chances are good that he will go on to read other books in the same series. This establishes him firmly on the path to becoming an avid reader. With so many great series to choose from, it will be easy to find another set of books when your child has exhausted the first. Soon your child will be looking for books by his favorite authors and will be well on the way to developing a love of leisure reading.

Start a book-of-the-month collection for your child. Once a month, take your child to the bookstore and let him choose any book he wishes, provided it isn't too difficult. Use the guidelines in Chapter 2, Matching Children with Books, to make sure the books you buy are within an easy-reading range. Put your child's name in the book, get him a bookmark, and set up a special place for his book-of-the-month collection.

Selecting his own books puts your child in the driver's seat. He decides what he wants to read and the books belong to him. The risk, of course, is that your child may pick out books that aren't accepted classics. If your child has a vague interest in books, it's likely that his selections will mirror other interests. Should your child be interested in racecars, his first few book-of-the-month selections are likely to be about cars. Likewise, a child who loves horses will seek out books on riding.

But to my way of thinking, reading is reading, whatever the topic. Perhaps at a later time you can share the classics with your child, but for now, the idea is to get him interested in reading. From the point of view of increasing your child's reading achievement, books about sports cars are just as good as traditional favorites. By virtue of spending some time leisure reading, your child's reading vocabulary will be richer and his comprehension better.

In time your child's reading interests will broaden. A major benefit of routine visits to bookstores is the exposure it provides your child to a wide variety of books. Bookstores, like your public library, have wonderfully broad reading menus. From books about model airplanes to the latest youth novel, everything is there. Browsing through the children's paperback books, your child is bound to pick something out of the ordinary. Such is the way new reading interests are born.

Set goals for recreational reading. Sometimes children need a bit of structure if they are to feel a sense of accomplishment. As a yardstick for success, a reading goal gives your child a concrete, reachable target.

Begin by setting goals on the low side, as realistic goals give your child targets he is certain to reach. Higher goals, like ten books a week for a third-grader, or two books a week for a sixth-grader, are overwhelming. If your child thinks he has little chance of reaching a goal, he probably won't try at all. Looking at a distant goal is discouraging and only adds to children's unwillingness to read.

It's been my experience that asking children to help set goals is a good way of getting them committed to a reading target. If your child is reluctant to read, he will undoubtedly set goals on the low side. Depending on how many books he suggests, some negotiations may be necessary to arrive at a suitable number of books. I usually respond to a goal that is much too low by countering with an offer slightly greater than what I believe will be the final goal, and then am prepared to compromise.

This is exactly what Edie's mother did. When Edie said she would read one book a month, the goal seemed far too easily reached by a third-grader. Her mother suggested three books; the final goal was two. Once Edie got into the habit of reading, increasing the goal to a larger number of books was not as daunting. Today Edie usually reads four books a month. No one sets reading goals anymore; Edie reads because she wants to.

Use a reading incentive program. Suppose you've tried all the reading spark plugs mentioned so far and your child still resists reading? What next? Every now and then, most children, even the best readers, go into a stall. Avid readers are interested in far fewer books than normal, while other children refuse to read altogether.

For times when you've tried everything and leisure reading is at a standstill, I have an extraordinary suggestion—a reading incentive program. Reading incentive programs are an accepted and highly successful practice in elementary schools. Sometimes reading incentive programs are schoolwide, and range from kindergarten to sixth grade, as the program in Durham, North Carolina, does (58). Other programs are aimed at a single grade, like the reading incentive program in my daughter's school.

Every spring the teachers in Susan's northern Virginia school select a theme—this year it's "Save the Dinosaurs." Last year it was Danny, a hippopotamus and the school mascot. The school is specially decorated, notes go home to parents alerting them to the upcoming events, and the contest begins. Children read books at home and volunteers check their progress at school by asking the children to read a short passage from each book and to answer a comprehension question or two.

Children earn prizes depending on the number of books they read. The children in Susan's school earn different prizes—a bookmark after one book; a certificate and stickers after three, six, and ten books; balloons after reading twenty books; pencils at thirty books; erasers for fifty books; a dinosaur button for the seventy-fifth book; and a book signed by the principal for the one-hundredth book. No one loses, since there are so many different benchmarks for success.

Tailor-made for first-graders, the reading incentive program produces results. It is the one time during the school year that teachers expect—and get—big jumps in reading achievement. Along with improved reading ability, teachers hope the children will develop a solid reading habit and continue reading for pleasure over the summer months.

Using the same idea, you can set up a reading incentive

program at home. Decide in advance how many books your child must read before a certain reward is earned. Like the incentives in Susan's school, start low and work upward, making sure each successive reward is within reach. Keep track of your child's reading by writing down titles and authors. If your child is younger, put the list on the refrigerator. For older children, keep the list in a notebook. The books you choose should be easy enough for your child to read on his own, or with very little help. Use the guidelines in Chapter 2, Matching Children with Books, to select books that are just right for your child's reading ability.

I can tell you from experience that reading incentive programs work at home. Having been convinced that the reading incentive program used by my daughter's school was a good idea, I adopted it for use with my own children. My only word of caution here is to think carefully before you commit yourself to a set of rewards. You must be prepared to follow through with your end of the incentive program. Be sure that the rewards you agree to are rewards you feel comfortable delivering.

I mention this because I told my daughter that for every ten books she read as part of our home reading incentive program, we would go to her favorite pizza restaurant. I was burned out on pizza long before Susan was willing to change our agreement! Although I ate more pizza than I wanted, overall the program was a great success. Susan read many, many books and, in the process, acquired an enthusiasm for reading that lasted long after the incentive program was completed.

EVERYDAY ACTIVITIES—
A NATURAL WAY TO GET READING PRACTICE

While reading books is the very best kind of practice, it's worth taking advantage of the reading opportunities that are part of your normal household routine. If you want your child to get lots of reading practice, you cannot afford to lose sight of the routine kinds of reading opportunities that pop up every day. Should your child be in the habit of reading for recreation, everyday activities will add to the benefits he is already getting from reading books. For the child who avoids books, everyday reading activities supply much-needed practice.

Each activity is an easy, effective way of weaving reading into your child's daily life. While the activities focus on a variety of materials, not one requires any preparation or preplanning. Not only are everyday activities great motivators and easy to use, they increase your child's reading vocabulary dramatically and improve his comprehension, not to mention perfecting the reading ability he needs to function on a day-to-day basis.

Breakfast cereal boxes offer a great opportunity for everyday reading practice! The sides of cereal boxes, which are designed to appeal to children, are a prime target of interest. The cereal my children beg me to buy in the grocery store has little, if anything, to do with taste (or nutrition), and everything to do with prizes. Cereal boxes with free prizes inside, or with offers of merchandise your child can order, provide real reading incentives.

Once your child has read about his prize or figured out how to order the set of drinking cups, pencils, and so forth, ask him to read some of the other things on the box. For older children, say third-graders and up, comparing ingredients from one brand to another is an excellent way to focus on nutrition. Moreover, your child will add a great number of words to his reading vocabulary and learn to make critical comparisons when he reads; both are important abilities for becoming an accomplished reader. Sometimes cereal boxes have recipes on them, which brings me to the next suggestion.

Reading recipes is lots of fun and your child has a good-tasting product when he's finished. Start simple. If your child has a favorite snack, like popcorn, this is the best place to begin. For younger children, instant pudding is easy and eliminates any risk of being burned. Cake and cookie recipes offer terrific reading practice for older children, as do easy recipes for casseroles and vegetable dishes. By-products of reading recipes include an improved ability to follow directions and a better understanding of the importance of paying attention to the correct order of events. These are critical comprehension abilities—abilities your child will be learning in the elementary reading program.

Don't go to the grocery store without giving your child responsibility for the grocery list. Ask him to tell you what is on the list and where to find it on the shelf. Make sure he crosses off products as they are put into your shopping basket.

Ask your child to hunt for the best bargains in the newspaper and in community shopping guides or other free weekly newspapers circulated in many communities. Comparison shopping with newspapers and shopping guides is a good way to develop your child's eye for bargains, to practice basic math skills, and to improve his reading comprehension, especially when it comes to comparing and contrasting information.

Reading television guides in the newspaper or commercially prepared viewing guides is another great way to give your child extra reading practice. Look for reviews of upcoming programs. Ask your child to read these reviews and recommend programs people in your family might be interested in watching. If you limit television viewing to certain times in the evening, reading television guides is a good way for your child to make more informed choices. What's more, judging quality is an extremely challenging reading ability, an ability that the elementary school reading program emphasizes in the fourth, fifth, and sixth grades.

When you need to consult a map, ask your fourth-, fifth-, or sixth-grader to read it for you. Explain where you are going and ask him to find the easiest route. Give your child the map while you are driving, so that he can tell you which roads to follow and which way to turn. An essential skill for getting along in society, map reading is taught in every elementary school reading program. The sooner your child learns to use maps, the better.

Magazines offer a wealth of reading possibilities. If you don't subscribe to a children's magazine, look for copies in your local library. These magazines are written specifically for children and have a variety of fun reading activities for children of the same age and reading level as your child.

Magazines for advanced readers and adults are also good sources of reading activities. Your kindergartner will have a wonderful time cutting out pictures of things that begin with each letter of the alphabet. Older children enjoy reading and discussing advertisements, the latest fashions, the newest cars, etc. With extra time devoted to reading magazines, you can expect your child's reading vocabulary to expand and his comprehension to improve, particularly when it comes to getting the gist of articles and remembering important facts and details.

Crossword puzzles are a wonderful learning activity, as are some board games. A variety of crossword puzzles are available for elementary school children of all ages and reading abilities. Not only are crossword puzzles great fun, they go a long way toward improving your child's reading vocabulary.

If your family enjoys board games, Scrabble, manufactured by the Selchow and Righter Company, is a good one, as it offers a combination of spelling and reading. Scrabble comes in several levels of difficulty, so that even the youngest elementary school child can play. In addition to acquiring a larger reading vocabulary, your child will spell better!

Coupons are another way to get your child accustomed to everyday reading. Give him the responsibility of organizing them in an envelope or container and ask him to make sure the right coupons go along with you to the grocery store. As with hunting for bargains in newspapers, reading coupons improves your child's ability to remember important facts and details, and to compare products critically. If your child would benefit from extra working of math problems, ask him to calculate the savings on a scrap of paper.

Have your child do the ordering from catalogs. This is a terrific way to give your child extra reading practice. Placing catalog orders requires many important reading abilities—following directions, locating information, figuring cost, filling out forms. All are valuable reading abilities—abilities your child needs to get along in society and to be a good reader.

Remember the newspaper! Newspapers carry information on upcoming events your child might be interested in attending, plus lots of sports and news. Talk with your child about the things he reads in the newspaper. Share your ideas and comments, and include your child, if he is old enough, in discussions of current affairs. By focusing on authors' points of view and biases, your child will develop reading abilities that are a fundamental part of reading instruction in grades four, five, and six.

Junk mail is something we all get. Why let it go to waste? Let your child open your junk mail; ask him to read it and decide whether it's worth keeping. Evaluating junk mail for its merit (or lack of merit) is an excellent way to give your child practice making judgments about the value of the things he reads. Your child will be working on these kinds of reading comprehension abilities in his classroom, and extra practice at home will be a great help.

If your child is starting first or second grade, take advantage of billboards and signs along the road. Ask him to read the names of businesses and talk about what billboards are trying to persuade consumers to buy. Once your child knows some of the words he sees on billboards and signs, work on finding these same words in other places in his environment—menus, advertisements in magazines, and so forth.

Children as young as kindergartners like to do their own ordering when the family goes out to eat. Whether it's a fast-food restaurant or a nicer place, it won't take long before your child is able to read the names of dishes and beverages he likes. While you're at it, ask him to tell you the price. If your child is older, say a second-grader, ask him to go one step further and add up the price of his meal.

Another great activity is to ask your child to write a short note to his grandparents, friend, aunt, uncle, or cousin. Holidays are particularly good times for notes. A Valentine, Halloween, or Thanksgiving card is always appreciated. Chances are good that your child will get a note or card in return, which makes for more good everyday reading practice.

The reading incentives described in this chapter will help your child develop the habit of reading for pleasure and get plenty of practice reading a variety of materials— library books, newspapers, magazines, pamphlets, recipes, do-it-yourself instructions, and so forth. In order to enjoy reading and to improve his reading ability, books and other reading materials must be well suited to your child's reading ability—not too easy and not too difficult. The next chapter provides ways of matching your child with the right books.

2

MATCHING CHILDREN
WITH BOOKS

There is always an element of trial and error when it comes to finding the right book. Looking is part of the fun— going from shelf to shelf in the library, picking up this book about horses and that book about George Washington, thumbing through the pages, reading a bit here and there to get a feel for the book's flavor. Some books click, others don't. Ultimately the choice is your child's, but you can assist him by tuning into his reading interests, helping him to locate books he can read comfortably on his own, and making sure books are available to him at home.

BOOKS FOR ALL READING INTERESTS

While your child's reading preferences are uniquely his own, years of experience matching children with books has shown that preschoolers prefer stories about family life, children their own age, and friendly, fantastic animals. By the time children are in the first grade, fairy tales and easy-to-understand humor are added to the list of favorites.

Fantasy is another genre that appeals to first-graders. Look for books that describe the adventures of talking animals, like *Fox All Week* (13), written by Edward Marshall, which recounts the adventures of fox and his friends, or books that feature friendly, talking monsters, like *Swamp Monsters*, written by Mary Blount Christian (14); both are included in the lively *Dial Easy-to-Read* series (15) for young readers.

Be sure to introduce your child to series of books that have been written for young readers. Many children enjoy the *Little Bear* books, written by Else Holmelund Minarik (16), which feature delightful forest animals. Books in the *Hello Reading!* series, written by Harriet Ziefert (17), and the *STEP into Reading* (18) books may also appeal to young readers who enjoy colorful pictures and lively, fanciful stories. These books, as well as the many other wonderful books available for beginning readers, will provide your child with pleasurable reading experiences and excellent reading practice!

Yet reading interests and intriguing stories aren't always at the top of a child's list when it comes to choosing books to read. While I was browsing through the books in the youth section of the public library, I stopped to watch a first-grader who was using a curious method to select books—she considered only the first and last pages of each book. Other features, including the title and topic, were apparently left out of her decisions. When I asked her how she decided which books were suitable to read and which were not, she told me that the most important criteria were how many words appeared on each page and how many pages were in the book. If there was too much print on the pages, or if the book was too long, she put it back on the shelf.

Many beginning readers prefer books that have one or two sentences on each page, are short (probably twenty-five pages or less), and have large, colorful illustrations.

These children are overwhelmed by books that cannot be read in one sitting. They want to read a book from cover to cover—finishing a book is energizing, satisfying, and verifies their perceptions of themselves as competent readers. The emphasis on shorter books that have plenty of illustrations will probably not be necessary beyond the first grade.

Although somewhat more challenging, the books in the *Nate the Great* series (1) offer first-graders and beginning second-graders a selection of mysteries—and they are also likely to enjoy reading about the adventures of the children who belong to the Small Potatoes Club in the series written by Harriet Ziefert (19) and coauthored by Jon Ziefert. Patricia Reilly Giff (20) has written a series, *The Kids in the Polk Street School,* that appeals to many children, perhaps because the stories are about believable children who have believable experiences. Another favorite of many first-through second-graders is the intriguing *Cam Jansen* mystery series (21), written by David Adler. Look in the front of the books in this series for enrichment activities your child might enjoy in conjunction with the stories. *The Fourth Floor Twins* series, also written by David Adler (22) and enjoyed by many young readers, recounts the adventures of twins who solve puzzling mysteries.

As children grow older, their reading interests expand. Third- and fourth-graders prefer adventure stories, realistic animal stories, books about sports, humorous books, fables, and series that chronicle the adventures of the same characters. Older children, say fifth- and sixth-graders, like to read adventure stories, humorous books, biographies, historical fiction, mysteries, books about the supernatural, and sports and animal stories.

Mature second-grade readers, and third- and fourth-graders, will relish books that have characters with super-human powers—like the extraordinary abilities of the young girl who performs astonishing feats in *Pippi Long-*

stocking, written by Astrid Lindgren (23), or the fantastic powers of Mrs. Piggle-Wiggle in the series of books about her written by Betty MacDonald (24).

Third- through sixth-graders will find humorous books particularly appealing. Look for books like those written by James Howe (25). Beginning readers may enjoy listening to the books that are written for more advanced readers read aloud. When we went on vacation last summer, I brought along a copy of Deborah and James Howe's book *Bunnicula: A Rabbit-Tale of Mystery* (26)—the story of the efforts of a dog and a cat to rid the household they live in of a vampire bunny—and used the time that we were riding in the car to read this book aloud. Everyone enjoyed the story!

Real-life adventures, like those in *Hobie Hanson, You're Weird,* written by Jamie Gilson (27), will be enjoyed by many third-, fourth-, and fifth-graders, and children who are interested in sports will enjoy reading *Tight End,* and the other books that Matt Christopher (28) has written. Books in *The American Girls Collection* (29), a series describing the lives of girls who lived in 1854, 1904, and 1944, may be of interest to third- through fifth-grade girls who like to read about the past. Look, too, for books like Patricia MacLachlan's (30) *Sarah, Plain and Tall,* a touching story about family life on the prairie, two children, their father, and a blossoming romance.

When you visit the public library, look for books by Judy Blume (31); her insightful descriptions of real-life, everyday experiences will be the favorites of many third-through sixth-graders. *Superfudge,* for example, explores the relationship between a boy and his younger brother with wit and sensitivity.

If you have an older elementary-age child, a fifth- or sixth-grader perhaps, who enjoys mysteries, look for the spine-tingling murder mystery *The View from the Cherry Tree,* by Willo Davis Roberts (32). While you and your child are in the library, introduce him to the books written by John Bellairs (33), an author who is known for his exciting Gothic thrillers, and Zilpha Keatley Snyder (34), who has written a number of books that older readers will enjoy.

All the books that I have described—and many more exciting, mind-engaging books written for elementary-age children—are readily available in your public library and on the shelves of the bookstores in your community. The books I have mentioned are meant to be guides, good places to begin when looking for books that your child might enjoy reading. Among the many good books for elementary-age children are the classics that you may have read as a child, books like Jim Kjelgaard's (35) *Big Red,* an action-packed wilderness adventure story about a young boy and his dog, and a plethora of delightful and exciting books written by new and talented authors. Paperbacks are relatively inexpensive, the illustrations are captivating, and they are written on all levels of reading difficulty—the number of books written for beginning readers has grown tremendously since we were children.

Conditions were different when I began teaching second grade in the 1960s. The children in my classrooms ranged in their reading abilities from those who couldn't name all the letters of the alphabet, to children who could read books written for fourth- and fifth-graders.

Knowing that the single most important ingredient for becoming a good reader is getting plenty of reading practice, I spent many hours looking for books that were suitable for my beginning readers to read for pleasure. The selection was limited, however, and I resorted to cutting up old reading textbooks and stapling stories together in order to make small booklets for the children to read.

Today, the youth section in most public libraries is a treasure trove for reading pleasure. There are plenty of good books written on all reading levels—books for younger readers and for older elementary-age children.

Librarians are knowledgeable and helpful, and children will find books on any topic—fiction or nonfiction—they choose to read about.

But just because good books are available and children know how to read doesn't mean they will choose to do so. A recent report of children's reading habits showed that half of the fifth-graders studied spent less than four minutes per day reading books. One of the great flaws of our educational system is reflected in the number of children who abandon books as a leisure-time activity.

Children's reading habits don't seem to vary much from those of adults. The amount of time the average American adult spends reading books is only five minutes daily. The discovery that, on average, adults and children spend approximately the same amount of time reading is startling—it suggests that reading habits are formed early on and, once formed, last a lifetime. When children set books aside for other pastimes, reading for pleasure is forgotten.

This is certainly a sobering thought, yet there is reason for optimism—if good reading habits are acquired during childhood, we can expect that our children will carry them into adulthood. This means that any extra effort that you put into helping your child to develop the habit of reading for pleasure today is likely to remain with him as he grows older.

FINDING THE RIGHT BOOKS

Learning about popular children's books is a good place to begin the search for the right books. Begin by consulting the librarian in the youth section of your public library. Not only does she have references describing popular children's literature, but she has an in-depth working knowledge of the books her young patrons enjoy.

One of the first categories the librarian is likely to mention includes award-winning books. Every year two awards are given to quality children's books—the Newbery Award and the Caldecott Medal. The Newbery Award is given for a distinguished contribution to children's literature, the Caldecott for an outstanding picture book. Both are awarded by the American Library Association and the Association for Library Service to Children.

Over the years I have shared Newbery and Caldecott books with children of all ages and have found that most of these books hold great appeal. Caldecott winners like *The Biggest Bear* (36) and *The Snowy Day* (37) are favorites year after year; I have read them many times to eager young listeners. On the other hand, just because a book has garnered a prestigious award doesn't necessarily mean that it's a good match for your child.

It is worthwhile remembering that these awards are given by adults based on adult criteria. The values of the adults who sit on panels judging books perhaps do not reflect the interests of the children who read them. So a medal winner, though it meets high standards of excellence, carries no guarantee that it will have a strong attraction for your child. Like any other book on the library shelf, award-winning books are worth consideration, but don't be disappointed if your child tells you he isn't interested in a medal-winner.

For any book to be a good match, it must capture your child's imagination. It seems to me that there can be no better judge of children's books than the children who read them. Children's Choices is such a hand-picked list. Made up entirely of the books that children cite as their favorites, Children's Choices is a product of the efforts of two groups—the International Reading Association and the Children's Book Council—and appears annually in the October issue of *The Reading Teacher,* a journal published nine times a year by the International Reading Association.

Books are grouped into five categories: All Ages, Beginning Independent Reading, Younger Readers, Middle

Grades, and Older Readers. A brief annotation accompanies each book, along with the bibliographic information necessary to locate the book in your public library or bookstore. (Use the information in Note 51 to inquire about obtaining a copy of the Children's Choices book list, which is distributed free of charge.) Depending on the resources your local librarian has at her fingertips, she may be able to supply you with copies of Children's Choices.

While you are talking to the librarian, ask to see a copy of the *Horn Book Magazine,* which reviews newly published children's books. And Beverly Kobrin's *Eyeopeners!* (52) provides recommendations for more than five hundred nonfiction books on a great many topics—mummies, alcohol, lasers, words, space, and so forth. Many of the books Kobrin suggests are suitable for reading aloud, and all are excellent references for youngsters whose teachers ask them to write book reports or research papers on a given topic.

If you are looking for a source of good read-aloud books, I suggest you consult a copy of Jim Trelease's *Read-Aloud Handbook* (53). Most librarians will have a copy of this book, and it is readily available in bookstores. In my view, Trelease's book has done more to encourage parents to read aloud to their children than any of the many highly publicized government reports and research findings. Trelease brings to his discussion of good read-aloud books the insight of a sensitive parent combined with a deep-seated love of literature.

One of the important features of read-aloud books is that they can be written for any level of reading difficulty, since adults do the reading and children the listening. Not so for the books your child reads on his own; in addition to capturing your child's interest, they must be written on a level equal to your child's reading ability. Books that are too difficult result in frustration, those that are too easy in boredom—which brings us to the question of how to find books written on a level of difficulty that makes them a suitable match for your child.

MATCHING BOOKS TO YOUR CHILD'S READING ABILITY

Once you find a few promising library books you'll need to decide which ones fit your child's reading ability and which do not. If your child has been bringing library books home from school, you may have already developed some sense of the kind of books he finds manageable. If you aren't sure, let me suggest an easy way to find books on a suitable level.

First look at the books you have found in the library and ask yourself which ones look like they will be easy, and which look difficult. Over the last decade or so there has been a dramatic increase in the number of easy-to-read books available to beginning readers. Easy-to-read books use common words, repeat the same words frequently, and have large print, easy-to-follow sentences, abundant pictures, and limited story length. Difficult books—those written for children with more advanced reading ability—use long words, limited (or no) illustrations, small print, lengthy sentences, and complex plots.

Having grouped books into easy and difficult categories, concentrate on those you believe are well within your child's reading range. Ask your child to read a sample passage and count the number of words he does not know. In their textbook for elementary reading teachers, Ekwall and Shanker (59) suggest that if children cannot recognize, or do not understand the meaning of, more than two words in one hundred, the book is too difficult.

Missing only two words in one hundred is a rigid criterion, yet there is wisdom behind Ekwall and Shanker's recommendation. Years of classroom practice have proven that children who miss more than two words in one hundred are likely to need a good bit of help in order to feel comfortable reading that book. The underlying reason has to do with reading vocabulary. When your child recognizes the majority of words in his storybooks, he is free to concentrate on understanding the story line. And, just as important, his self-esteem increases when the books he reads are well within his capacity.

Successfully reading one book becomes an incentive to read another and so on, which is exactly what one wants to happen. Reading difficult books has the opposite effect. Trying to read books that are too hard does more harm than good—it is a wet blanket dampening your child's flame of enthusiasm. Hard books are frustrating, take a tremendous amount of effort, offer little or no pleasure, and often result in a sense of failure. The net result: your child's interest in books wanes, lessening his enthusiasm for reading. If this isn't bad enough, while reading difficult books, your child spends so much time figuring out the words that his comprehension inevitably suffers and his fluency (the normal rhythm we want our children to have when they read) is destroyed.

Ekwall and Shanker go on to suggest teaching your child to judge books for himself by holding up a finger for every problem word. When two fingers are up, the book is too hard. Some easy-to-read books don't have enough words to use a one-hundred-word sample. In this case, ask your child to read a whole page. If he misses more than two words on a page, the book is going to have too many words he doesn't know.

Counting mistakes puts the entire emphasis on your child's word knowledge, since it is assumed that children who know the words will also be able to understand what they read. Most of the time this is a valid assumption, but not always. If you suspect your child might not be able to understand the ideas in a book, you might want to help him learn something about the subject of the book before he reads on his own, or you might want to help him when he reads.

Reading sample passages from books is a sort of trial-and-error approach to finding a good match. I prefer this method because it gets children involved in a book right away and allows decisions to be based on a child's actual reading performance. If, however, you would also like to have some numbers to fall back on, I recommend using a readability formula.

Readability formulas are used by teachers and book publishers to estimate a book's difficulty. These formulas result in a number that is supposed to represent the "grade level" of a specific book. Books with a third-grade readability are roughly appropriate for children capable of reading on a third-grade level, books with a fifth-grade readability for children reading on a fifth-grade level, and so on.

Of the many formulas used to assign readability, not one is a precise measure. Among the most popular readability formulas is a graph developed by Edward Fry (54) that yields reading grade scores from first grade through college. Scores are based on the average number of syllables and the average length of the sentences in three different one-hundred-word passages. The two averages—number of syllables and length of sentences—are used to plot the difficulty of a book. Your child's teacher is likely to have a copy of the Fry Readability Graph. If not, you can use the information in Note 54 to obtain a copy of this formula.

As with any estimate, readability formulas do not yield precise measures of reading difficulty. They do not take into account whether or not your child has any interest in reading the book, how enticing the illustrations are, or whether your child can understand the text.

Most formulas rely solely on measures of word difficulty and sentence complexity to estimate reading grade levels.

Books with short words and short sentences are assigned low reading grade levels; books with long words and long sentences are given high reading grade levels. Readability formulas usually result in two numbers that indicate reading level: the first number refers to the grade in school and the second number to the months spent in a grade. For example, 2.1 refers to the second grade, the first month; 5.5 to the fifth grade, the fifth month.

Many publishers of children's books indicate the readability levels of books on the backs of covers or on the pages preceding the beginning of the story. *James and the Giant Peach* by Roald Dahl (38), an engaging book about the adventures of a boy who encounters wonderful characters when a huge peach grows in a treetop, has an RL 6 (RL refers to readability level, 6 to the reading grade level) printed in the lower-right-hand corner of the back cover. This number suggests that it would be a good match for children in the sixth grade. Readability levels are a guide intended to measure the suitability of a book for children who might choose to read it for pleasure. Consequently, certain good readers in the fourth and fifth grades will find this book suitable for leisure reading.

On closer inspection, you will find that *James and the Giant Peach* is a wonderful read-aloud book. The adventures of the warm, engaging characters in this book will be enjoyed by many younger elementary-age children. When my daughter was in the first grade, her teacher read it to the class, a few pages at a time, every day after lunch. The children loved it!

Certain publishers and certain series of books will indicate a range of grade or age levels that are intended to help parents select suitable books for their children. The *STEP into Reading* series, published by Random House, uses this method. This extensive series of easy-to-read books includes Step 1, written for preschoolers and first-graders; Step 2, for first- through third-graders; and Step

3, for second- and third-graders. Many children will read a book from this series from cover to cover in just one sitting. Look for this information in the upper-right-hand corner on the cover.

Printed on the back covers of the books in the *I Can Read* series, published by Harper & Row, and in the *Dial Easy-to-Read* series, published by Dial Books for Young Readers, are recommendations for a range of ages that may enjoy the books. Children may be able to read the books for pleasure, or to listen to the books read aloud by their parents. *Hello, Mrs. Piggle-Wiggle* by Betty MacDonald (24) is recommended for children ages six to ten; *Pippi Longstocking* (23) is recommended for children ages seven to eleven. These two books will provide hours of reading pleasure for third-, fourth-, and fifth-graders, and hours of listening enjoyment for younger children whose parents read aloud to them.

Sometimes children recognize all of the words in a book, but the complexity of concepts outstrips maturity, range of experience, or educational background. When this happens, comprehension falls short. This may happen when children can read well above their grade placement in school.

Meiko stands out in my memory because, at six, she loved to read joke books written for fourth- and fifth-graders. The interesting thing, her father told me, was that Meiko never laughed at the jokes. She just read joke after joke until the book was finished, and then looked for another book. It wasn't that Meiko had problems with comprehension. When she read books within her maturity and experiential range, Meiko did well. But when she read books written for an older, more mature audience, she ended up "calling" the words out loud without any real appreciation of their meaning.

This is not to say that books outside a child's personal experience should be avoided, but that the mental gymnastics required by some conceptually complex books may not meet your child's needs. If your child is interested in reading books that deal with subjects beyond his background experiences, you can be certain that your child will have some comprehension problems. However, the desire to read such books provides a wonderful opportunity to enrich your child's knowledge of the world.

Such an opportunity presented itself when Terrance brought home a copy of Betsy Byars's (39) book *The Two-Thousand-Pound Goldfish*. In order to understand this spellbinding book, the reader must appreciate the complexity of underground sewer systems in large cities. Such an understanding is necessary because one of the book's central figures is a large goldfish who lives in the storm sewers of a large city. Living in a rural farming community had not provided Terrance with the background knowledge that he needed to enjoy this book. However, his mother helped him develop an understanding of storm sewers by taking him to the library to locate books on them, and talking with him about the need for such systems. As a result, Terrance enjoyed the book, became more knowledgeable about the world beyond his rural home, and enlarged his speaking and reading vocabularies.

The two methods I have described—counting mistakes in a practice passage and using a readability formula—aren't intended to put a ceiling on your child's capacity to read a particular book; each method will provide you with enough guidance to select books in the right ballpark. The final judgment, however, must rest on your child's reading interests. Children who are intensely interested in reading about a certain topic will put in the extra effort necessary to read books that are theoretically "above" their reading grade level.

When nine-year-old Valerie became the proud owner of an eight-week-old calico kitten named Fluffy, she read every book she could locate on cats, many of which were above the level of difficulty that she was accustomed to. Still, Valerie enjoyed the books she read and continues to be an avid reader of animal stories. Today's young readers are sure to be enchanted by the wonderful pictures and the useful information in Colleen Stanley Bare's (40) book *To Love a Cat*. Like Valerie, they will put forth the effort to read this thoroughly delightful nonfiction book. In the final analysis, then, any book your child is excited about reading and capable of appreciating is a good match.

MAKING BOOKS AVAILABLE

It's crystal clear to me that children who become avid readers have grown up in homes where plenty of books and reading materials are available. The best way to ensure ample opportunities to read at home is to build a personal library for your child. Personal libraries mean book ownership, and I know my children have had more than one argument over who has the "right" to a favorite book. Arguments usually end up with the owner taking a stand: "This is MY book." "My book" doesn't rule out lending books to family and friends—it means that the special books in a child's personal library are shared by consent. Once this basic rule is understood, each person has the right to save those books he values most.

When Jim Trelease talks about good read-aloud books, he says a book worth reading as a child should be worth reading again as an adult (53). Books with staying power are the ones your child will keep, which doesn't necessarily mean saving all the classics. It means holding on to those books that, for whatever reason, your child finds pleasurable over a long period of time.

One of my most treasured childhood memories is of a book of poetry. Although I didn't know it at the time, there are few classic poems for children in my book; what made the book enchanting for me, though, was the fascinating things those poems told about. Sharing this book with my children, I remembered again the pleasure I found in the goblins, dragons, mermaids, and gypsies who live inside its covers. My children have their own favorite books. The books they choose to keep in their libraries will be their literary bridges between childhood and maturity, a permanent sort of literary connection with the past.

Escalating cost is one of the major drawbacks to building personal libraries. We have sidestepped some of the cost by giving our children books for birthdays and holidays and by asking relatives and friends to do the same. Cindi's mother did this when I asked her what Cindi might like for a birthday present. "Oh, that's easy," she replied. "Cindi just loves books." When we went shopping for presents, my son made the selection. "Oh, Mom," Brian said, picking a book from the shelf, "this book is great. Cindi will just love it." And she did. Then, when Brian had a birthday party, Cindi gave him a copy of Jean de Brunhoff's *Babar the King* (41), which is the current family favorite.

Paperbacks sold by school book clubs are a good source of relatively inexpensive new books. If your child's school participates in a book club, you'll receive a monthly advertisement of books costing between one and four dollars. My daughter's school routinely sends these book club advertisements home. Susan makes the selection and the teacher does the ordering. You can get information on paperback book clubs from the Children's Book Council (55).

And let me share a terrific idea for free books: an annual "book exchange," something my daughter's elementary school holds each spring. All of the children in the school bring books they no longer wish to have in their personal libraries. Used books are exchanged free of charge. Children are asked to bring as many as ten books—paperback or hardcover—they wish to swap. Two days are set aside for the children to bring in their books; the book exchange is held in the school library on the third day. For each book brought to the school, children receive a coupon that is good for one book in exchange. Children go home with an armful of "new" books to be relished and kept for years, or enjoyed and brought to the book exchange the following year.

If your child's school doesn't have something similar, a book exchange is worth getting started, especially since they promote book sharing across a broad range of ages and reading interests. Organizing a book exchange takes a good deal of time and energy—much more effort than any one of us could provide single-handedly. Such a project could perhaps be undertaken by a cooperative of parents, the Parent Teachers Association (PTA), or an interested civic group.

Building a personal library means finding bookshelves to house your child's collection. While shelving can be an expensive investment, it need not be. Painted boards atop bricks make for serviceable, inexpensive shelving. Putting books on shelves with the spine facing outward will help your child quickly locate titles, although this is not a necessity. I've gotten into the habit of stacking on one end of a shelf oversized books that are much too big for the makeshift shelving we have at home. This kind of horizontal book storage means that my children must sort through the stack each time they want to find a particular big book. More often than not, they come across several interesting books they weren't originally looking for. Sometimes they stop to leaf through the pages of an old favorite before going on to find the book they want, and sometimes they add books to the read-aloud stack for the evening.

Leave room on your child's shelves for books from your public library. The library is a rich source of literature and it's absolutely free. I can think of no better way to reinforce the value of reading for pleasure than to make regular visits to your library and to set an example by reading yourself.

Next time you visit the public library, get your child a library card if he doesn't already have one. Not all libraries use cards these days, but those that do are anxious to include young patrons on their list of card-holding borrowers. Our town library asks only that a child be able to write his name to qualify for a library card. After my daughter got a library card, the next visit saw my son, whose head didn't even come above the counter, carefully writing his name on a borrower's application.

Children who have their own library card develop a sense of responsibility and of independence. Responsibility comes with returning books on time and in good condition; independence comes in exercising control over selection. A library card says in a clear, tangible way: I am a reader; my reading preferences count; I know how to care for books.

3

SHARING BOOKS
WITH CHILDREN

How can you help nourish your child's love of books and
commitment to leisure reading? Here is where sharing
books with your child is especially helpful. Unlike reading
spark plugs, which act as incentives for children who typically do not read, or who have little or no interest in books,
book sharing is a means of linking the books your child is
reading to his everyday life experiences with artistic
expression, with imagination.

Sharing books at home is a concrete way of showing
your child how much his family values good books and the
power of reading. Not only will your child get more enjoyment from the books he reads, but he will choose to
spend more time reading in his leisure hours. One of the
things we've learned about children who read for pleasure
is that they are better readers than children who do not
choose reading as one of their recreational activities.

There is no substitute for leisure reading. No other activity, inside or outside the classroom, contributes as much

to improving fluency, word knowledge, comprehension, and speed. The number of new words your child learns each year is evidence of how important leisure reading is to overall reading achievement.

Third- through sixth-grade children learn approximately 3,000 new words each year. Usually we think of school as the place where children learn all the words they need to know, but 3,000 new words a year is well beyond the scope of an elementary reading program. Where do children learn these many words? Some are taught in school, of course, but the majority are learned unintentionally, often through leisure reading.

In a landmark assessment of learning to read in America, the Commission on Reading (60) recommended that third- and fourth-grade children spend at least two hours per week reading recreationally. This is equivalent to spending slightly less than twenty minutes a day reading books, a figure well within reach of every child. Children who spend modest amounts of time reading books, magazines, even comic books are far ahead of children who do not read for pleasure. Leisure reading is so important that as little as ten minutes a day makes for a recognizable difference in a child's reading ability (61).

By calling for more leisure reading I do not mean to imply that children's pastimes need be weighted heavily toward reading. Instead, I am suggesting that most children need a balance among recreational activities. The kind of child I have in mind is not a loner who finds in books the social outlet he is unable to find with friends. The "bookworm" who reads instead of spending time with classmates and participating in sports is, for the most part, a fictional character from a past that provided fewer diversions.

Today's avid reader is much different. When he is asked to name the leisure activities he likes best, reading is not usually at the top of his list. Avid readers mention activities like spending time with friends, pursuing sports, watching television, playing video games, and so forth.

Even though reading isn't the avid reader's favorite pastime, these children obviously enjoy reading and do so regularly. Perhaps avid readers have a long-standing commitment to reading for pleasure because they are surrounded by people who value books—especially people at home. We cannot impose on our children our own attitudes toward reading, nor can we force them to become lifelong readers. We can, however, fashion our family life in such a way that our children come to appreciate the pleasures of reading.

When you share books with your child, he is encouraged to pick up books and to read them on his own. Listening to you read aloud, your child comes to appreciate the power of a good story. Seeing *you* reading for pleasure, he learns the value of recreational reading. Setting a good example is particularly important since so much of what your child sees around him discourages his spending time with books.

As your child grows older, his world is increasingly dominated by hype designed to sell products. Bright colors, fast action, loud music, unrealistic physical feats: the list is almost endless. Your kindergartner or first-, second-, or third-grader is bombarded with a mind-boggling array of media blitzes. No portion of your child's world is exempt— from advertisements for twenty-five-dollar toys, to action-packed cartoons, to fast-food restaurants that cater to kids.

Certainly the situation is more intense for your older elementary-age child. As being part of the crowd becomes more and more important, what's "in" to do and to own (seventy-five-dollar sneakers or the latest tape player, for example) commands a large share of your child's attention, not to mention a sizable chunk of your wallet. All of these things send messages to your child—but not the kind of messages that suggest that reading is an important, enjoyable form of recreation.

It's easy to turn on the television, sit back, and let the producer show you how he imagines fictional characters might look, dress, and act. Television doesn't have to be—but most frequently is—a passive recreational activity. While there are many excellent, mind-engaging programs for children, a great number are mind-deadening. The sight, sound, and motion carry your child into a story. Someone else has already done the creating and imagining; your child has only to soak up the action like a sponge.

There is no doubt that television has a special hypnotic lure. The majority of fifth-graders spend four minutes or less daily reading books at home. Four minutes a day is paltry by any standard, yet few would judge television-watching as unimportant in children's lives. On the average, American children spend approximately two hours a day watching television. The National Assessment of Educational Progress (62) reports that in 1984 slightly over one-fourth of the nine-year-olds questioned watched more than six hours of television each day.

Six hours a day! That translates into approximately 828,000 nine-year-olds who are spending one quarter of each and every day in front of the television set—an astounding figure. These nine-year-olds do not represent an atypical sample of youngsters. The National Assessment of Educational Progress is our most prestigious system of national testing, and the figures quoted are an accurate reflection of American youth.

It's not that television-watching is necessarily harmful, although many experts suggest otherwise. Programs can be highly stimulating, and children who read well often watch a good bit of television. Estimates put the time good readers spend viewing television somewhere between ten and fourteen hours a week. Watching ten to fourteen hours a week is one thing. Spending forty-two hours weekly in front of the television set is another entirely. Sitting glued to the television set after school, on weekends, and on holidays is a sure path to becoming not only physically unfit but mentally dependent on someone else doing the thinking.

It will come as no surprise, then, that watching six or more hours of television a day has proven to be related to low reading achievement. Let there be no doubt—children who spend extraordinary amounts of time mesmerized by television do not read nearly as well as children whose parents limit television viewing.

The connection between poor reading and watching too much television has more to do with the things that children who are watching television cannot do with their leisure time. If they are to become skilled readers, children need to practice, and leisure reading is the best kind of practice your child can get. When children choose television in favor of reading books, they miss out on the kind of practice necessary to perfect their reading ability. Without practice, learning to read becomes more difficult, children fall behind, and failure is the ultimate outcome.

It's worth remembering, too, that learning to read requires a tremendous amount of effort and practice throughout your child's elementary-school years. I sometimes forget just how vital practice is for young learners, particularly when it comes to learning what adults take for granted. When my daughter was six years old, she took a series of swimming lessons offered by our town recreation department. One of the strokes she learned to do was the crawl. In order to do the crawl, one must float, kick properly, move the arms (while keeping the hands cupped), and breathe, all at once. Coordinating motions is the greatest problem. Children who can do everything separately end up with mouths full of water when they try to coordinate motions. It is a question of getting enough practice so that all of the motions fit together smoothly and become automatic. For my daughter, the by-product of a summer's worth of swim practice was a fluid swimming motion, and movements carried out automatically.

Dancers call this "muscle memory." It is what happens when a person practices something so much that the action can be performed without consciously thinking about carrying out the individual parts. Like learning to swim, an outcome of reading practice is the kind of effortless reading we think of as skilled reading. Book-sharing activities give your child the opportunities necessary to get the kind of reading practice he needs, while at the same time showing your child how much you value reading as an enjoyable and rewarding pastime.

SUSTAINED SILENT READING

If you want to give your child time to practice reading, and if you believe, as I do, that your child learns by example, ask everyone in your family to spend a short period of time reading each day. Teachers call this Sustained Silent Reading (SSR). A proven classroom technique, SSR shows that children who spend just a few minutes each school day in uninterrupted reading make outstanding gains in comprehension and reading vocabulary.

Alan Rossman (63) describes a project in which children spent from seventy-five to eighty minutes each week using SSR in school. First-, third- and fifth-graders who were given extra time in class to read made such gains in vocabulary, comprehension, accuracy, and speed that reading was transformed from a fragmented, slow process into a smooth, efficient one. These children no longer needed to put a great deal of effort into coordinating individual reading abilities but could concentrate instead on the important ideas and concepts presented by the authors.

SSR is an extremely simple and highly effective means of giving your child reading practice at home. All you need to do is set aside a time, perhaps fifteen or twenty minutes, when everyone in your family will read. SSR is a perfect match for families with busy parents and children. It requires no preparation, yet it gives your child a chance to see firsthand the importance you place on reading. Using SSR as a family reading time gives everyone a book to talk about, which brings us to the next two suggestions.

PREVIEWING

Previewing works in much the same way as movie advertisements do on television. Ads give prospective moviegoers a sense of the movie's flavor with the hope that viewers will exchange the living room sofa for tickets for a seat in the local theater. Previewing, as the movie advertisers know, has a powerful and persuasive influence.

I'm constantly explaining to my children the reasons we won't be going to see some of the movies advertised on television. Our most recent discussion revolved around why a movie with a penchant for violence and the occult was a poor choice. It took a great deal of explanation from me to undo what a commercial had done in less than thirty seconds.

To some extent, the influence of commercials speaks to the power of television as a means of shaping our children's reactions and perceptions. But it also suggests that giving prospective moviegoers a taste of what they will see on the silver screen makes greater the desire to follow up on ads.

Previewing books operates on the same principle. The idea is to pique your child's interest by telling him a little bit about a book and then letting him take the initiative and read the book on his own. Just like the movie advertisements, you want to tell your child just enough to capitalize on his interests, but not so much that he is turned off by a lengthy explanation. Hitting the high points, or giving your child a brief overview of the story, is all you need do. You want to highlight those things in the book you believe will appeal most to your child. From there on, it's up to your child to decide whether or not he wishes to pick up the book and read it.

I was reminded last summer when I was looking through some young-adult selections in our town library that children rely a great deal on previewing when they recommend books to one another. While browsing I overheard two fifth-graders talking about Thomas Rockwell's *How to Eat Fried Worms* (42). One of the boys had read the book and was recommending it to his friend. "This is about a kid who eats worms. There's a real great part in here where this kid says he'll eat a worm a day. He makes a bet for fifty dollars that he can eat fifteen worms. It's great!" He pointed to a cover showing four boys looking over a large, apparently juicy worm on a silver tray. That did it. His friend was hooked. What a wonderful way to spend leisure summer hours at age ten!

While children are extremely persuasive when using previewing to recommend books to each other, and although my daughter likes to read books I tell her a little bit about, this may not be the case with your children. The librarian in the youth section of our city library offered this useful piece of advice: "If your children are like mine, just leave the books lying around. They'll pick them up on their own. Don't say anything." She went on to say, "I always found with my three boys that saying 'This is a good book' was the kiss of death. No one ever read it." Here is a lady who knows how to get her children to read. Previewing didn't work for her, but she found a method that did.

If you leave books sitting out, be sure to leave a few beside your child's bed. The hazard, of course, is that your child might choose to read instead of sleep, but I see no problem with reading before bed, provided children don't stay up so late that they are tired the next day. The backseat of the car is another good place to leave books. When you plan a trip, bring along some books your child might be interested in reading by himself, in addition to good read-aloud books your child will enjoy listening to.

BOOK TALKS

Anything that is a part of the fabric of family life is worth talking about, books included. Previewing sets the stage, but the real grist for discussion comes out of reading. The advantage of book talks is that they don't have to be scheduled or planned in advance. Riding in the car, preparing dinner, getting ready for bed—all are good occasions to talk about books.

Book talks needn't take a great deal of time, either. Conversations can be as lengthy or as brief as fits the situation. They can be as simple as your child remarking how much he is enjoying the book he is reading, or as involved as a discussion about the beliefs and values of characters in the story. Simple or elaborate, book talks bring books to life. But there are other ways to make books come alive. Using drama and art are among the best.

ADDING A DRAMATIC TOUCH

Acting comes naturally to children. As an integral part of make-believe play, very young children act like Mom and Dad, dinosaurs, pirates, and other real or imagined characters. When they reach elementary-school age, children are more subtle in their use of drama, but acting the part of different characters is no less important. The third-grader playing with her doll is an obvious example, or the fourth-grader with his collection of model airplanes. Even older, say sixth-grade, children hold fast to the pleasures of putting themselves in someone else's shoes.

Not long ago, we took our children to a friend's house

for dinner. Her eleven-year-old son was spending the evening with two other boys from his sixth-grade class, and I was concerned about how we were going to entertain our two young children. I shouldn't have worried. No sooner had we stepped in the door than my friend suggested that our children might like to play with her son's collection of wrestling figures. Out came a large-sized model wrestling ring, along with more wrestling figures than I knew existed. Each eight-inch plastic figure was just the right size for the ring. My two children had an evening's entertainment.

Later, I learned that my friend's son was taking wrestling lessons and hoped to qualify for the team when he entered the junior high school; his heroes are the real-life men the figures represent. In a sense, those toy wrestling figures were a way for her son to step into the shoes of his heroes.

Dramatizing storybooks works in much the same way. It gives your child a chance to act out his own interpretation of a character, an episode, or a story. There are four possibilities here: improvisation, pantomime, puppets, and masks. While improvisation and pantomime require no preparation time, puppets and masks call for some preliminary artwork.

Improvisation is a good place to begin since your child has probably had lots of experience improvising during play already. My youngest child makes up whole conversations among imaginary characters. He creates some of the dialogue from his own imagination, some of it comes from bits and pieces of family life, and some from school friends and neighborhood children. It wasn't too long ago that I walked into the living room to find him standing on the chair, imaginary sword in hand, calling "Stand aside, dragon!" Using improvisation as a book-sharing idea is a natural extension of this kind of dramatic play. No script is necessary, only your child's imagination and a good memory for his favorite book.

Any book works with improvisation, provided the story captures your child's interest and imagination. When Summer was in the first grade, she read an easy-to-read book called *Bony-Legs* (43). This is a story about a little girl, Sasha, who is captured by Bony-Legs, an old witch. Bony-Legs lives in a hut that stands on chicken feet, and she eats little children. Sasha befriends Bony-Legs's animals, who help her to escape the witch's grasp. Written on a mid–first-grade level, *Bony-Legs* is an exciting, action-packed story.

When Summer dramatized this story, she screwed up her face and spoke in a mean, shrill voice as she imagined Bony-Legs would. When playing the role of Sasha, Summer was kind, smiling, and sometimes afraid. In a sense, Summer was "trying out" different character roles to see how each felt and to find out if a character was a good fit for her personality. When your child uses improvisation to dramatize favorite stories, he may decide, as Summer did, to put himself in the place of different characters. Much personal growth can result from this kind of experience.

Your child will learn how it feels to be someone or something else, and he'll gain tremendously important insights into the story. These insights are building blocks for the advanced comprehension abilities he will need as a mature reader. One of the things skilled adult readers do is analyze stories, reports, and newspaper articles from the point of view of the author, also taking into account views the author may have left out. These abilities are crucial for detecting biases and understanding when an author is trying to sway his reader's thinking. While such a level of understanding is well beyond children as young as Summer, the kind of thinking that goes into the role-playing Summer did lays the foundation for the sophisticated comprehension abilities that will develop later.

Like improvisation, pantomime is a dramatic way to make books come alive. While improvisation is suitable for children of all ages, though, pantomime is especially good for older children—third- through sixth-graders, for example. The only rule is that words must never be used. Ideas are conveyed with facial expressions and body movements. Younger children who have a difficult time with the silence of pantomime enjoy watching older siblings silently acting out characters, actions, and events.

Here is a terrific opportunity to turn pantomime into a guessing game the whole family enjoys: ask your older children to pantomime emotions while younger siblings guess how the character feels. Specific action-oriented scenes from a book, like setting up camp for the night or looking for a lost animal, are good for guessing, too.

Of the four possible ways to dramatize books, my children have had the most fun with puppets. We have a gingerbread man puppet on our refrigerator right now. Our gingerbread man is the simplest kind of puppet—a piece of paper cut out to look like a gingerbread cookie, with colored eyes and mouth, taped to a stick. A child of any age can handle a gingerbread man. Paper-bag puppets are especially fun for children in the five- to seven-year-old range.

Napkins make great puppets, too. Make napkin puppets by crumpling a napkin into a ball. Place a second napkin over the ball and fasten a rubber band around the whole thing. Fasten a string to its head to make the puppet move. Napkin puppets have a sort of ghostly appearance which makes them perfect for Halloween, but they can be readily transformed into nearly any character. My daughter added two black eyes, a red mouth, whiskers, and two pointed ears to make a convincing cat.

Older children like body masks. Made of an old sheet, a large cardboard box, or paper bag, body masks cover your child from head to toe, creating a rather dramatic effect. Body masks transform your child instantly into anything or anyone he wishes—perhaps this accounts for their universal appeal. Not only are they terrific for dramatizing stories, but they are a wonderful means of artistic expression. If you have older children at home, body masks are sure to be a hit.

Many of the puppets that captivate children and adults today are strange-looking creatures with large noses, over-sized heads, and fantastic bodies. Still, they are lovable forms of artistic expression because they represent the unique personalities of their creators. The great thing about puppets and masks is that they needn't be beautiful or expensive, only expressive. Puppets and masks will enhance your child's artistic expression, and will provide him with wonderful opportunities to explore emotions and to improve his use of spoken language. Shy children will be energized by puppets and masks; outgoing children will have an appreciative audience for expressing their ideas.

Makeshift stages—a card table turned on its side, for example—are easy to come by. Making puppets and masks are good indoor activities and offer hours of creative fun. Your elementary-school child can make them on his own, freeing you to do other things. But most important, puppets and masks provide a stimulating forum for sharing your child's versions of his favorite books.

USING AN ARTISTIC EYE

When we think about reading we normally have in mind engaging our children's minds with literature. But there is also an artistic eye in the mind that is waiting for expression. Art and literature are natural partners. We know readers create pictures in their minds of the characters and events in the books they read. Art is a concrete means of "verbalizing" and capturing those pictures. Teachers have known this for years and continue to connect the pictures that books make in children's minds with children's artwork in illustrations, murals, and posters.

Mobiles, collages, and posters are good ways for your child to express his feelings about the book's best- or least-liked character, the most exciting event, the setting, or the saddest part. Not only is art stimulating, but it is an activity your child can do anytime. Rainy days, evenings at home, days when your child is ill and home from school, vacations without planned outings—all are super times to get out the crayons, Magic Markers, or paint. If the books in your child's personal library need protection, making colorful, descriptive book covers is lots of fun. Or perhaps your child would like to decorate a door in the house by illus-trating something special from a favorite book. This, too, is great fun!

Sometimes children like to draw pictures about the books they read and then write something special—a sort of caption—about the picture at the bottom of the page. After reading *The Story of Annie Oakley* (44), third-grader Hollie drew a picture of Annie with her gun. Under the picture Hollie wrote, "Annie shooting game for her family to eat." This book is a biography, one in a series recounting the lives of famous Americans. It was first published in 1956, and Hollie read the original hardcover edition.

Where did Hollie get such an old book? Probably not in the public library, although there are many good biog-raphies there. This book came from the attic. The series of biographies, along with a companion series on historical events, is part of Hollie's mother's personal library, saved from childhood. I can think of no better way to model a lifelong commitment to literature than by giving our chil-dren a part of our past bound in the pages of our childhood library.

READING ALOUD—A SPECIAL WAY TO SHARE BOOKS

Of the many ways to share good books with one's children, reading aloud is among the most influential. Reading books aloud combines many experiences we know are important for a child's growth—the security of being close to a protective adult, the soothing effect of hearing another human voice, engagement with a fascinating story, the stimulation of vicarious experiences. Delores Durkin, a well-known authority on reading, says about reading aloud, " . . . the most successful (and enjoyable) way to interest children in acquiring the ability to read is by reading to them frequently from carefully chosen books" (64). Part of the magic of reading aloud lies in the book, part in the act of sharing between reader and listener, and part in the way parents model good reading.

What will your child learn when you read aloud to him? First and foremost, your child will learn to love good books. Your child will come to think of reading as a pleasurable, worthwhile leisure activity. When your child listens to you read aloud, he is completely involved in the unfolding story. He doesn't have to worry about recognizing words or turning pages. He is free to let his imagination transport him wherever the story goes.

As your child listens to stories read aloud, he learns what good, skilled reading sounds like—a smooth, fluid, spoken rendition of print. This fixes a goal in your child's mind of how he should sound when he reads, providing him with a way of knowing when he himself is reading well.

You can also expect your child to learn a great deal about language. Children whose parents read aloud to them have superior vocabularies and use more complex sentences than children whose parents do not. They also learn that good readers pronounce the words so that the rhythm of the language is preserved and the intent of the author is conveyed.

By watching their parents read, young children pay closer attention to print on the page. They come to realize that tiny black marks are the things to concentrate on, that readers begin from the left and move to the right of each line, that readers start from the front of a book and from the top of each page. This information seems rudimentary, and it is, but such basic knowledge is the scaffolding that permits other, more sophisticated information about reading to fall into place. Children in possession of this information find learning to read a pleasurable, successful experience. Children who do not have a firm understanding of these fundamentals are obliged to learn them before making even the most primitive progress toward reading.

While it is true that children are never too young to enjoy stories read aloud, it is equally true that adults are never too old. Terry Lovelace describes the discussion of ideas that came about when she spent Friday afternoons reading to patients in a nursing home ranging in age from forty-four to ninety-two years old (65). Lovelace believes that her reading enhanced the lives of the patients, and gave them a focal point for talking with one another—in effect, acted as a catalyst for contact among patients who normally kept to themselves.

The only known time during a school day that a particularly rowdy class of high school students in rural North Carolina kept quiet was when their English teacher read to them. Reading aloud is so influential that it transcends language differences in classrooms. Children who speak little or no English are captured nonetheless by the stories read aloud by their English-speaking teachers.

We know that the spellbinding quality of reading aloud is a magnet attracting children young and old. This doesn't mean, though, that the same books are good for all ages. Sometimes books that are just the right fit for older children are over the heads of younger audiences. Even when children are separated in age by as few as two years, as my children are, there is no guarantee that because a book is right for one child it will also be a good fit for the other.

My daughter is currently listening to her father read *Prince Caspian*, the second of seven books in the *Chronicles of Narnia,* by C. S. Lewis (45). An absolutely terrific book, it's exciting, imaginative, fast-paced, well-written—all the things that make for a wonderful experience with literature and a great read-aloud book. Yet as wonderful as this book is, my son, Brian, gets only limited pleasure from listening to the story. He always wants to be in the same room when Susan's father is reading aloud, but he doesn't sit spellbound as Susan does. Instead, Brian plays with his toys, listening to the story with one ear and hopping on his dad's lap when there's a good picture.

It's not that Brian is unable to pay attention or is uninterested in hearing stories read aloud. Brian and this particular book are mismatched. While *Prince Caspian* is just right for Susan's age and range of experience, it is too mature for Brian. So Brian snuggles up to his father or to me, and listens intently to a different kind of story, one more in keeping with his level of development.

While Susan prefers long books like *Prince Caspian,* Brian enjoys shorter, colorfully illustrated stories. Like most young children, Brian likes listening to the same read-aloud storybooks many times. Rereading favorites is especially important because preschoolers seem to absorb stories bit by bit. As children become familiar with read-aloud storybooks, they spend more time talking about their favorites, ask more insightful questions, and seem to develop a better understanding of the story lines. It will come as no surprise when I say that a preschooler's earliest attempts at reading often come out of listening to familiar favorites. If you have a preschooler, you have probably watched with amusement as your child pretended to read by turning the pages of familiar storybooks and saying the words just as he had seen you do. Preschoolers learn a great deal about books when they imitate skilled readers— how to turn the pages from the front of the book to the back, how to differentiate between illustrations and written words, and how to associate words with the pictures on the pages, for example. Perhaps even more important, the joy that comes from pretending to read much-loved stories strengthens the foundation for a lifelong commitment to reading.

A good read-aloud book offers opportunities for parents and children to think about the story. There are so many exciting episodes and enchanting characters in the *Chronicles of Narnia* that talking about the events, about evil and benevolent creatures, and about the children whose adventures are being recounted is a natural part of the read-aloud experience, as it should be. There is little evidence that merely reading a story from cover to cover does much for a child's appreciation of literature, or for his reading competence.

It's not just *reading* the book; it's sharing the story that counts. Sharing a read-aloud experience means doing other things along with reading—pointing out the title, asking about the meaning of pictures, defining purposes for listening, reacting to episodes, forming opinions. We want our children to be active participants in the read-aloud experience, not passive bystanders.

In order to encourage your child's active participation you must know something about the story *before* you read it aloud. You may want to read entire short books—longer ones can be skimmed for a sense of overall story content. Once you are familiar with a story you are ready to read it aloud.

Suppose you borrowed *A Toad for Tuesday* (46) from your public library. This is a wonderful book about a toad who is captured by a hungry, but lonely, owl. The illustrations are marvelous and the story line exciting. Find a comfortable chair, curl up with your child next to you, and begin by pointing out the title and talking about the picture on the cover. Lawrence De Fiori has drawn an intriguing picture in which he has captured the sense of the book. A large owl sits glaring down at a small, rather frightened toad. The toad, who is sitting at a table with a teapot and two cups, is looking up at the owl with a tentative expression. A bold circle is drawn around Tuesday on a calendar in the background. Talking about this wonderfully expressive picture will generate enthusiasm for the story and get your child immediately involved in the read-aloud experience.

Continue to talk about the book as you read it. Listen to your child's comments and help him to focus on important ideas and events in the story. Toward the beginning of this story there is a wonderful passage in which the owl and the toad are talking inside the owl's house, far up in a tall tree. The owl asks Warton, the toad, where he is going on such a cold winter day. Warton replies that he is going to visit his aunt. The owl then tells Warton that he, Warton, can expect to remain in the owl's house, at least until next Tuesday. The tone of the owl's voice is ominous, and Warton is on the alert. This is the perfect place to ask your child what he thinks the owl might do on Tuesday.

Predicting events is an excellent way to promote comprehension since your child must think back to what has already happened in the story and use this information to predict how the story is likely to unfold. Perhaps you would prefer to talk about how Warton feels, trapped high above the ground, and focus on affective aspects rather than on story sequence. Talking about a story as you read it creates the kind of interest that often spills over into a desire to retell the story from memory.

RETELLING READ-ALOUD STORIES

Along with a heightened appreciation for good books, there is a great deal of personal growth that comes from retelling read-aloud stories. As a way of extending the read-aloud experience, retelling is a natural next step for children of any age. Prereaders "tell" stories spontaneously by leafing through the pages of books while commenting on the action. But even this early form of retelling is viewed by the teller as a personal sharing experience. The last parent I witnessed interrupting a preschooler in the midst of this kind of retelling was soundly told, "No, let me do it!"

One of the wonderful outcomes of retelling is your child's desire to put himself in the place of the characters. I remember how completely absorbed Peter was with Maurice Sendak's *Where the Wild Things Are* (47). This story of a naughty little boy, Max, and his dreamlike adventure with a collection of kind but fierce-looking creatures is especially intriguing—no child can resist the wonderful charm of Sendak's monsters. At the opening of the story Max's mother tells him that he is too high-spirited and orders him to his room. Retelling this part of the story, Peter substituted some of his mother's favorite phrases, like "I've told you before to quit running in the house" and, "If you don't calm down, you'll wear yourself out." As Max, Peter used a defiant tone when recounting how he, Max, told his mother that he would eat her up. Peter gave a wonderful description of the monsters, explaining how brave Max was to tame them.

Sometimes children retell a story with great attention to the smallest details, as Peter did. At other times children choose to include only the major events. Regardless of how generally or specifically a story is recounted, the storyteller is sharing his personal experience with literature. This kind of experience is extremely important for developing reading ability and for learning to appreciate the pleasures of literature. Children who retell stories focus on salient story features, like the setting, characters, theme, and sequence of episodes leading to the end of the story. Collectively, these story features make up what is called a "story structure," a sort of schema for predicting the progression of good stories.

Children between ages four and six can usually remember the setting, beginning, and outcome of a story. Older children remember more complex elements, like a character's reactions, and different attempts to resolve the story. The more children understand about story structure, the less they must depend on the physical presence of the book to help them recall events, and the better they are able to understand what they've read. Good readers have a uniformly excellent understanding of the structure of stories that poor readers do not. Without a knowledge of how stories are structured, a child has no mental road map to follow and often becomes confused in the intermingling of characters and events.

Like retelling, all of the book-sharing suggestions in this chapter provide ways of establishing a family reading climate where your child's life is enriched by literature. Sharing books with your child sends a clear message: reading is an activity that requires personal involvement, demands thoughtful reactions, and results in tremendous enjoyment. Now that you have captured your child's interest in books and are sharing with him his experiences with literature, it's time to focus on how and where the elementary reading program fits in, and how you can work constructively with your child's school to make him a better, more eager reader.

4

THE READING PYRAMID

"**W**hat will you learn now that you are going to school?"
I asked a bright-eyed first-grader. "I'm going to learn to
read," was Michael's enthusiastic reply. After looking into
Michael's classroom, I saw the reason for his certainty
about learning to read. There were words everywhere—
written on the chalkboard, fastened to bulletin boards,
printed on moveable charts, attached to the walls. There
was a large, colorful set of ABC's on the wall, a tape re-
corder with books and cassette tapes in a corner, an ample
supply of paper and pencils on the shelves, and an assortment of books for the children to enjoy on their own
or for the teacher to read aloud to the class.

Michael's teacher believed that the students in her classroom should be provided with an abundance of printed
and writing materials (books, magazines, newspapers,
pamphlets, paper and pencils, etc.) to use and to enjoy.
Many teachers and many reading authorities share the
view of Michael's teacher that the children in elementary
school classrooms should be surrounded by opportunities

to read, write, listen, and speak. There is less agreement among educators, however, on the use of approaches for the teaching of reading.

Of the many approaches used to teach reading in American elementary schools, the basal reading approach and the whole-language approach are the most frequently discussed. These two approaches—basal and whole-language—are the center of a raging controversy among educators, and chances are good that you will hear your child's teacher mention them. Although the basal reading approach and the whole-language approach are quite different, each has been shown to be an effective means of teaching reading to elementary-age children.

THE BASAL READING APPROACH

This is a highly structured approach to the teaching of reading—the word "basal" refers to the foundation or essentials that are necessary for learning to read. If the basal reading approach is used to teach reading in your child's elementary school, the school will have purchased a set of teaching materials (called a basal reading program) from one or more publishing companies.

As a self-contained teaching approach, the basal reading program includes all the materials your child's teacher needs to teach reading—reading books (called basal readers), workbooks, tests to gauge how well children are mastering the program, and an amazing array of extra teaching materials like posters, puppets, oversized books, supplementary reading materials and worksheets, and so forth. Teachers are to use these materials to teach a series of reading abilities, tailored by each company to the basal program it publishes, at each grade level.

As you can imagine, basal reading programs are costly. Few schools can afford to purchase all of the materials offered by publishers of basal reading programs. The most frequently purchased, and the most basic, items include reading books, workbooks, and manuals explaining how to use the materials.

Learning activities might entail the reading of a story (or portion of a story) in a basal reader, including the teaching of reading abilities like comprehension, vocabulary, and phonics, and the completion of the pages in a workbook that reinforce the abilities that the children are learning. Other activities—writing a story, reading books for pleasure, playing a learning game—extend children's experiences with print beyond the stories in the basal readers.

The basal approach to the teaching of reading is so well established in American elementary schools that the Commission on Reading called it the driving force behind classroom instruction (60). This approach has been the backbone of American reading instruction since before the turn of the century. It was the most popular teaching approach when your parents were in elementary school, and you probably learned to read with a basal program when you were a child as well. Do you recall reading a series of books, the easiest of which read something like "Look, look, look. Can Mary run?" Books for beginning readers then had lots of pictures and fewer words. Harder books were, for example, collections of stories, often about the same family or group of characters. If you remember learning with books like this, you were taught to read with a basal reading approach.

Basal reading books aren't exactly as you remember them, however. Basals have changed considerably since the time you and I learned to read. The stories are more interesting, words aren't repeated as frequently, sentences make better sense, and illustrations are more enticing and represent a variety of different ethnic groups and lifestyles.

Most basal reading programs purchased from publishing companies use five books in the first grade: three pre-primers, one primer, and one first reader. Preprimers are short, paperback readers with limited vocabulary and simple stories. The primer and first reader look like regular books in as much as they have normal-length stories, do not repeat words excessively, have more print than pictures, and are bound with a hard cover. The majority of basal reading programs include two basal readers for children in the second grade—a 2–1 book that is to be read during the first half of the second grade and a 2–2 book that is to be read during the second half of the year. Likewise, there are usually two third-grade books—a 3–1 reader for the first half of the school year and a 3–2 reader for the second half of the third grade.

While the primary grades (kindergarten through third grade) concentrate on teaching your child the fundamentals of reading, the upper grades (fourth through sixth grade) focus on developing advanced reading ability. In the fourth through sixth grades, most—but not all—basal reading programs use only one book per grade. If your older elementary child has two basal readers in his classroom, one will be a book of literature, the other a skills-oriented reader.

These books concentrate on teaching your child to use reading as a learning tool. By systematically introducing advanced comprehension and study skills, basals strive to develop the upper-level reading ability your child will need to move into junior and senior high school, to become a productive wage-earner, and, eventually, to become a literate adult.

THE WHOLE-LANGUAGE APPROACH

The word "whole" refers to the integration of the teaching of reading, writing, literature, and oral language. The whole-language approach teaches reading in a natural or holistic manner which encourages children to explore print freely, to write, to read about, and to discuss the subjects that are of interest to them. Children read a wide variety of library books, newspapers, magazines, pamphlets, reference books, and so on.

Unlike the basal approach, in which prepackaged materials shape instruction, learning in whole-language classrooms arises out of the needs and interests of the children. Each whole-language classroom is a unique reflection of the creativity and characteristics of the children and the teacher. Using themes of interest to children, teachers provide activities that will help the children in their classrooms to become independent learners. A fifth-grade class, for example, may read and critique newspaper articles on the problem of air pollution, carry out research in the library on the subject, write their own versions of newspaper articles, and share them with their classmates. The children in a first-grade class might create their own oversized books to read, write in a personal log each day, play word-learning games, read easy library books, and so on.

The whole-language approach fosters cooperation, not competition. Instead of dividing children into groups of good, average, and poor readers, as is common in classrooms in which the basal approach is used, groups in whole-language classrooms have specific short-term purposes—to complete a special project, to dramatize a story, or to share books on a special topic, for example. Children work together—in small groups, in large groups, or with a learning partner—and act as resources for one another. Teachers read good literature aloud, and the children share their impressions of the plot and talk about important vocabulary. Time is set aside each day for uninterrupted silent reading. Known as Sustained Silent Reading (SSR), this is the same book-sharing activity that I have suggested you try at home. Teachers use book talks (another technique recommended for use at home) to discuss the books that the children have chosen to read during SSR. Book talks focus on the new information and the new vocabulary in library books, and on the pleasure of reading for recreation. Sometimes children note the troublesome parts in books, then meet in groups to share their strategies for inferring meaning and for learning new words.

A fundamental feature of the whole-language approach is the teaching of reading and writing together. Teachers may ask the children in their classrooms to write at least once every school day. The focus is on conveying ideas, emotions, and attitudes through written language. The use of correct spelling and grammar comes when children edit and polish the first drafts of what they have written. They should be encouraged to read their own writings and those of their classmates.

When my daughter was a first-grader, her teacher used many of the methods that are part of the whole-language approach. The children in my daughter's classroom wrote each day, dictated stories to their teacher, wrote their own versions of stories that the teacher had read aloud, and kept a daily log of their activities. Spelling and punctuation were not corrected; the children were to concentrate on expressing their ideas. Each child had a personal diction-ary—several pieces of lined paper stapled together—in which they entered words that they used frequently. The results are impressive: my daughter loves to write, creates well-structured stories, and has learned a great deal about reading that she might not have learned without the free-dom to express herself in writing.

UNDERSTANDING
THE READING PYRAMID

The average elementary school reading program is set up like a pyramid, with each of a total of seven tiers repre-senting a grade in school. The bottom four tiers represent the primary grades (kindergarten through third grade), and the top three tiers the upper elementary grades (fourth through sixth grade).

Each tier acts as a support for the one above it—reading abilities developed in one grade form the basis for learning in the next. If your child does well in kindergarten, he will most likely have a good foundation in the first grade. Good, steady progress in the first grade provides a solid base to support learning new reading abilities in the second grade, and so on.

Tiers toward the bottom of the pyramid are larger than those at the top, since learning to read occupies a great deal more time and covers a larger number of fundamental reading abilities in the primary grades than in the upper grades. When your child reaches the top of the pyramid he will be able to read library books on his own, and will have the abilities necessary to read subject-matter textbooks in math, science, social studies, and health. Equally important, your child will be ready to meet the challenges of the junior and senior high school years that lie ahead.

When the reading pyramid works as it should, your child makes steady, upward progress. How quickly he climbs to the top of the pyramid depends on how rapidly your child learns to read at each tier (or grade). To stay on track your child must complete the basal readers assigned to his grade in school, or must develop the reading, writing, and language abilities taught each school year in the whole-language approach. When this happens, your child makes average progress by moving up the pyramid in step with his classmates.

The average rate of progress becomes the standard your child's teacher uses to measure how well your child is achieving. Children who are above average are perhaps a step or two up the pyramid from everyone else. Children who make average progress move up the pyramid one tier for each year spent in school. Children performing below average are behind their classmates, a step or two down from the rest on the reading pyramid.

Average progress places your child squarely in the middle of his class, and well on his way to becoming a skilled reader. We tend to talk a lot about "average progress." It is as though we believe that somewhere there is an "average" child sitting behind a desk making absolutely "average" progress learning to read. I've never met such a child. No child I've ever encountered makes completely "average" progress all the time. From time to time children move a little bit more quickly, other times a bit more slowly.

Because the level of reading ability associated with average performance is likely to be the yardstick your child's school uses to measure his achievement, it is important to have a clear sense of what an average child is like. As a means of illustrating average progress I'd like to tell you more about Michael, the little boy I mentioned at the beginning of this chapter. A successful learner, Michael is a good example of how the reading pyramid works when children move along at an average pace.

CLIMBING THE LOWER TIERS
OF THE READING PYRAMID

I first met Michael when he was in the first grade. I remember him being a cute little six-year-old, about average height and weight, with dark hair and dark eyes. Michael had done well during kindergarten—having learned his ABC's, how to write his name, to recognize colors and shapes, to read a few words, and to remember the sounds of certain initial letters in words. He entered first grade with a solid background for climbing the reading pyramid.

The basal reading approach—the predominant means of reading instruction in American schools—was the method used by the teachers in Michael's elementary school. When Michael entered the first grade, he was ready to start reading in the first preprimer. He finished the third preprimer early in the year and went on to read the primer and first reader.

By the end of first grade Michael knew enough about phonics to figure out the pronunciation of many of the new words in his storybooks. He knew most of the sounds associated with single, initial letters in words—like the sound of the **l** in **lady** or the **p** in **pocket**—certain letter-sound combinations that appear in the middle and at the end of words, and some endings like **ing, ed,** and **s.**

Michael could remember the sequence of events in stories, arrange words in alphabetical order, recall both facts and details, follow simple written directions, and select the best title for a story. If you stop to think about it, you'll realize that Michael learned a staggering amount in the first year of school.

As Michael moved through the second and third grades he continued to make average progress. He read the two basal books each written for second- and third-graders. In the second grade Michael built on the foundation he had acquired in the first—he learned to recognize the letter-sound combinations of certain groups of letters, such as **str, pl, br, oy, sh, th,** and **ck;** to locate certain details that supported the ideas in a story; to read some contractions, such as **isn't, can't,** and **I'll;** to predict the events in some of the stories he read; and to recognize words that signal cause and effect.

In the third grade he built on the foundation laid in the second. By the end of the third grade, Michael could use phonics to sound out any word with reliable letter-sound patterns, and he was capable of using all the common word endings, like **er, est, ful, less,** and **ous** and most possessives, like the **boy's** ball. Also included in Michael's newly acquired reading abilities was a solid foundation in comprehension. Before Michael went into the fourth grade he could read and follow directions several steps long. He had refined his ability to find and remember important facts and details, and he was able to focus quickly on the central theme of anything he read, identify multiple causes of an event, and paraphrase the material he read. Michael also knew how to use the table of contents in a book, how to write simple reports, and how to carry out school projects.

During the primary grades there comes a time when children have mastered a sufficient number of reading abilities to begin to feel comfortable reading library books on their own. This is a critical point for all children, and you should watch carefully for this stage in your own child's development. Comprehension is the first clue you should look for; using phonics to sound out unknown words is the second.

If your child can explain the contents of the books he is reading, recall basic information, and understand the reason that certain events in stories take place, comprehension is in place. You know that your child can sound out unfamiliar words without help from you when he mumbles new words to himself until he gets the right pronunciation, and then continues reading.

If you can see a surge in the amount of time your child spends reading for pleasure, it is a clear indication that your child is approaching (or has reached) this pivotal point. Leisure reading increases because, for the first time, your child is able to read independently, on his own, anywhere he chooses—sitting in the living room, riding in the car, lying in bed. If your child knows only a few words and doesn't have the phonics ability to sound out new words on his own, he needs someone by his side when he opens a book to read. Without an adult nearby who can help with the words he doesn't know, he is unable to read even the simplest storybooks. But with a larger vocabulary and solid phonics ability, two major stumbling blocks have been eliminated, allowing your child to read library books without extra assistance from you.

I knew my daughter had reached this point when the flashlights in our house started disappearing. Susan asked for a night light; I turned down her request, recalling that she had been sleeping without a night light for several years. Besides, I explained, she shared a bedroom with her younger brother, who was always there to keep her company should she be afraid of the dark.

I later realized that it wasn't fear of the dark that had prompted Susan's request. She wanted enough light to read in the bedroom. Each night after I put the children to bed, Susan had been taking a storybook from its hiding place under her pillow and reading aloud to her younger brother, Brian. Not hearing loud noises coming from the bedroom, I assumed both children were asleep. When I learned that Susan was reading well past their bedtime I understood why I had been seeing such dark circles under my children's eyes in the morning.

Now I was faced with a dilemma. I didn't want to squelch Susan's desire to read to Brian, nor did I want to dampen Brian's interest in storybooks. On the other hand, late-night reading was a problem since both children were often too tired to get much out of the next day. Moving reading time to just *before* bed—rather than just *after* bed—resolved the problem, at least on most nights. Although changing the time worked, I think some "after-hours" reading still goes on from time to time. On those nights when Susan chooses to read an extra few pages after lights out, I've decided not to say anything, as long as it doesn't again become an every-night routine.

Early in the second grade Michael reached the pivotal point where he changed from a child who needed the teacher to tell him unknown words into one who could work out the pronunciation of words by himself. He had learned enough about phonics to use it the way it is intended, as a means of learning new words in stories. Because Michael's comprehension was good, he was capable of enjoying the books he read. From this time forward, Michael was in a position to learn to read at a faster and faster pace.

Because he could read library books comfortably without assistance, he read a great many books and got a lot of reading practice. The more he practiced, the better he read and the larger his vocabulary grew. Michael completed the third grade a competent, independent reader equipped to grasp the sophisticated abilities that would be introduced in grades four through six.

READING ON THE
HIGHER TIERS OF THE PYRAMID

During the primary school years, Michael had a reading lesson every day. In the fourth through sixth grades, Michael's teacher taught formal reading lessons about three times a week. Basal readers were used less frequently because subject-matter textbooks, like social studies and English books, became the major tools for teaching reading. In a very real sense, reading instruction went beyond the basal reader—the heart of the program which was used in Michael's school during the early grades—to extend to all types of reading materials—fiction and nonfiction books, newspapers, magazines, pamphlets, etc.

There is a sort of ripple effect favoring children like Michael who make average progress. Good reading ability and good performance in subject-matter areas complement each other. It works like this: If your child reads well, he is able to comprehend his subject-matter textbooks and complete assignments. As a consequence, your child profits from instruction in subject-matter areas and makes average (or better) progress in math, science, health, and social studies. At the same time, your child increases his reading ability as a result of the practice he gets as he reads his textbooks.

The mutually beneficial relationship between reading and subject-matter learning is most critical when your child has reached the higher tiers of the reading pyramid. In the early elementary years, learning in math and other subjects doesn't depend a great deal on reading skill. For the most part, if your child has basic computation skills (knows how to add and subtract) and has a good general knowledge, his achievement in subject-matter areas will be satisfactory.

However, as subject-matter textbooks begin to use more and more words to explain concepts and impart information, reading ability becomes increasingly more important. By the third grade, it is difficult to keep up in subject-matter areas without average reading ability. Beyond fourth grade it's nearly impossible.

Average fourth-, fifth-, and sixth-graders have the reading ability they need in order to learn from their subject-matter textbooks; poor readers do not. While making ordinary reading progress doesn't guarantee good grades in other school subjects, teachers and reading authorities agree that the kind of steady, forward progress Michael made cannot take place without solid reading ability.

By the end of sixth grade, Michael had learned to recognize the syllables within words, and his reading vocabulary was extensive. He could read the newspaper, popular magazines, and a variety of books, fiction and nonfiction. Michael had expanded and improved his reading comprehension so that he could enjoy an assortment of different literary forms—short stories, essays, poetry, plays, mysteries, and so forth. He knew how to infer characters' emotions, differentiate between fantasy and reality, relate the ideas and experiences he read about to those in his own life, make generalizations, and summarize the material he read.

Michael was well on his way to reading with a critical eye. He knew something about how to identify an author's point of view, and he was able to draw conclusions, detect mood and setting, find bias, identify propaganda, and judge the overall quality of the things he read. Clearly he was prepared to extend and refine these sophisticated comprehension abilities as a secondary school student.

When his teacher asked him to write a report, Michael was able to use the card catalog to locate relevant resources, take notes from references, and synthesize his findings. In his social studies class, he read the subject-matter textbook in the way the text was intended—as a learning tool. Michael knew how to use the glossary to identify unfamiliar words, and he could interpret bar graphs showing population changes across the years, read maps showing the routes of explorers, answer the study questions at the end of the chapter, and complete homework assignments.

By the end of sixth grade, college was still far away for Michael, yet he had developed the foundation he would need to continue to profit from classroom instruction and eventually to go on to college, should he choose to do so. And Michael had gained something else—a positive attitude about school and a good self-image.

He knew he could learn, and he knew he was successful, and so he approached school with the knowledge that he had the skills necessary to do the job well. Because he had faith in his own ability, Michael was open to new experiences, and he was willing to try something a second time if he ran into trouble the first.

After leaving the sixth grade, Michael continued to do well in school. I expected this outcome: After all, the reading pyramid gives an advantage to children like Michael who master the reading abilities taught in each grade. Because Michael went to junior high prepared with the reading abilities he needed, the effect of the reading pyramid continued to work to his advantage throughout junior high and into senior high school.

After high school, Michael chose to go to college. Your

child may decide to get a job, attend a junior college, or go to a technical school. That's his decision. What's important is that your child has the opportunity to make that decision. If he makes the kind of reading progress Michael did, the odds are very high that your child will stay in school and will be a good reader. And when he graduates from high school, he will have the reading ability to do whatever he chooses with his life.

We want our children to become informed, thoughtful, literate adults, to turn out the way Michael did. The elementary school reading program lays the foundation for literacy. The junior and senior high school years put the frosting on the cake by refining reading ability. By climbing the reading pyramid on schedule and in step with his classmates, your child develops a positive attitude toward reading and a belief in his ability to learn. This combination—a proven track record and a good self-image—is the bedrock for learning throughout life and one of the fundamental ingredients for success.

5

TALKING WITH YOUR CHILD'S TEACHER

The single best source of information about your child's day-to-day progress in school, meetings and discussions with teachers are indispensable. Two or three times a year your child's teacher will invite you to a parent-teacher conference in order to let you know how your child is progressing. At other times during the school year, you may want to ask his teacher to set aside some time to discuss your child's work. Having children of my own in school, and having spent over twenty years in education, I have spoken with a great number of teachers in many different circumstances.

I have gradually come to appreciate that successful conferences with teachers, even successful phone calls, take a bit of preparation. Your child's teacher prepares by collecting samples of your child's work and deciding what she wants to tell you about his development. As a concerned parent, the best way for you to prepare is to decide before talking with the teacher what you want to know about your child's reading ability.

WHAT TO ASK THE TEACHER

More than once, I have finished talking with my child's teacher only to realize I had forgotten an important question. I've learned to avoid this problem by making a list of the questions I want to ask and bringing it with me to the conference. I don't always need to consult my list, but I have it with me in the event that I do.

I am offering you my list below, knowing that you will want to add questions specifically related to your own child. Only five questions long, my list covers the basic information you'll need to know about your child's reading progress. I like to ask the questions just as I've written them; you may feel more comfortable putting the questions in your own words. What's important is to get the right kind of information, which is exactly what my five questions are meant to do.

Question 1. On what grade level is my child reading? Determining your child's reading grade level is the best way to measure your child's progress. If your child is in the fourth grade and his teacher says your child is reading fourth-grade books, fine. On the other hand, if your child is reading below his grade level, you'll want to know at which level he is capable of reading.

It seems logical that report cards should give mention to something as important as reading grade levels, but this isn't always the case. Whether or not your child's school makes it a policy to inform you of his reading grade level is something that teachers, administrators, and school board members often decide. I know of schools that provide this information, but I also know of schools in which children are assigned to "levels" like 1A. These levels correspond to reading grades, but you'll probably have to ask the teacher to explain what the levels mean.

I remember talking to Robby's parents about such a mix-up. They had been getting report cards all year that described Robby's reading level as 1A, 1B, and so on. During parent-teacher conferences Robby's teacher said he was making progress; therefore it didn't occur to Robby's parents to request an explanation of his reading grade level. As the end of the school year drew near, a note came home saying that Robby hadn't made the kind of progress he should have and that the school was considering retention.

Robby, it turns out, had made such slow progress that he had failed to complete even half of the reading program at his grade level. If Robby's parents had been notified earlier in the year that Robby was behind his grade level, they would have been able to help him catch up by working with him at home. Finding out about slower-than-average progress at the end of a school year is too late.

If you are uncertain of what the teacher is telling you, don't hesitate to ask for more detailed information. An answer like "1A" often isn't clear enough. If you want to pursue this question further, ask the teacher what level basal reader (assuming the school uses a basal reading series) your child is reading from. If the whole-language approach is used to teach reading in your child's school, ask the teacher to tell you the level of difficulty of the library books your child is capable of reading. With this information you are ready to ask the second question.

Question 2. Looking at your class, would you say my child is an above-average, average, or poor reader? While reading on grade level is a good barometer by which to gauge overall reading progress, it isn't always an accurate reflection of how your child is doing in comparison to the other children in his classroom. Reading books written on grade level might be "average" for the children in one classroom, "above average" in another, and "below average" in still a third classroom. This makes asking how your child fits into his particular class a worthwhile question.

Knowing how your child is classified in the eyes of his teacher is immensely helpful. His teacher's evaluation will tell you how well your child measures up to his classmates. Because so much of your child's self-esteem is tied to how he perceives his standing among his friends, this is extremely important.

I remember visiting a classroom in an inner-city school where the highest achievers were reading "on grade level," reading the right books for their grade in school, and the rest of the class was reading below grade level. I also spent time in a suburban classroom where many of the children were reading books written one, two, or three grades above their grade in school. When I asked one little fellow reading on grade level in the urban school if he was a good reader, he answered, "Sure, you bet."

The children reading on grade level in his classroom thought of themselves as successful readers, and they were. This view of themselves wasn't shared by children reading on grade level in the suburban school. They thought of themselves as being a bit weak in reading, even though they weren't. Clearly, what sets the standard for good reading and for poor reading from your child's point of view is how well he reads in comparison to his friends.

There is another reason to ask about your child's standing among his classmates: reading grade levels don't tell the whole story. Suppose it is late May and your child's third-grade teacher says he is reading on a third-grade level. Ordinarily, this would mean that your child is making average progress. But suppose that your child's school uses the basal approach to reading and that your child had only just begun the first of *two* third-grade readers. If this were true, he would probably fall into the "below-average" group. Third-graders making average progress should be finishing the second of the two third-grade basal readers (the 3–2 reader) in late May, not beginning the first third-grade book (the 3–1 reader), which means your child is almost a year behind. Should your child's school use the whole-language approach, he ought to be reading library books written for skilled third-grade readers, not books that are appropriate for mature second-graders or beginning third-graders.

By combining the information you've gathered from the first and second questions, you should have a clear sense of your child's general reading ability. Now you are ready to focus on specifics.

Question 3. How well does my child understand what he reads? The single most important reading ability, comprehension, should be asked about. Everything else might be in place—a large vocabulary and knowledge of phonics—but without good comprehension no other ability is useful. If problems with comprehension arise, you need to know immediately.

As a general rule, younger children will have fewer problems with comprehension than older children. The primary reason for the difference is this: authors of books for beginners stick more closely to everyday life experiences familiar to children than do authors of books for older readers. Because younger children already know a great deal about the topics about which they read, comprehension doesn't require a great deal of effort. Even as adults, the more we know about a subject, the easier it is to understand the author and the less concentration it demands to do so.

If you know a lot about history, reading a book on the post–World War I era is relatively easy. You probably know the bulk of the terms you need and have the background knowledge to make sense out of the points the author is making. Young readers encounter much the same situation—they have many background experiences on which to draw. Their major goal, then, is learning the words in storybooks.

Suppose someone hands you a copy of a law that the United States Congress has recently passed. Unless you have had some prior experience with legal matters, trying to read and make sense of legislation is no simple task. Understanding what that law means will take a great deal of effort because you don't have much relevant background experience.

By the time your child is a fourth-grader, he will be reading about many things beyond his personal experiences. Once he is standing on the upper tiers of the reading pyramid, your child can no longer compensate for weak comprehension by relying on his background knowledge. Now he must use his ability to consider the meaning of the words he reads. As a consequence, you may first become aware of comprehension difficulties toward the end of third grade or the beginning of fourth grade. This is too late! The foundation for good comprehension is built early on and it's important to keep tabs on your child's progress from the start. This way you avoid the onset of comprehension problems by giving your child extra help whenever little problems arise.

Question 4. What are my child's greatest strengths in reading? The focus here is on the kinds of reading abilities at which your child excels. Knowing your child's strengths allows you to skip over information he has and to concentrate your efforts at home on the things he needs to improve.

Question 5. What areas does my child need to work on? How can I help at home? Equipped with the answers to this question, you can plan the kinds of home activities that will best benefit your child. His teacher will be happy to share some suggestions with you, and there are many good learning ideas in the phonics, vocabulary, and comprehension chapters of this book. The ideas are easy to make and easy to use. Many are adaptations of games and activities with which you and your child are already familiar—tic-tac-toe, puzzles, bingo—and are to be completed in short periods of time.

The experiences I have had working with my own children, and helping other parents to teach their children, have convinced me that effective home learning activities must be different from, must amplify the paper-and-pencil lessons children complete in their classrooms. Activities should be action-packed, mind-engaging, and fun—learning new words by circling them in newspapers and magazines, improving phonics by collecting different words with the same letter-sound combinations, and increasing comprehension by arranging the frames of comic strips into the correct sequence.

These activities, and the other activities in this book, have proved effective. To administer them requires no specialized training, and will make your child a better and more avid reader.

An extra question. There is one other question I would like to share, although it doesn't deal directly with reading: I always want to know about my child's work habits. Specifically, I ask whether my child can follow directions, complete classroom and homework assignments, and work independently. Sometimes children get behind in school simply because they don't finish assignments, or because they cannot work independently. If my child is having trouble with work habits, I want to know.

TIPS FOR TALKING
TO YOUR CHILD'S TEACHER

If you come to the parent-teacher conference with the right questions but ask them the wrong way, the conference will not pave the way for the kind of positive working partnership you want to establish. Here are a few tips, many given to me by other parents or learned through personal experience, about how to talk with your child's teacher.

Bring a positive, supportive attitude. A positive attitude is the most important contribution you can make to any conference. When you begin on a positive, supportive note, the teacher will return your friendliness, sensing your willingness to work with her. A good attitude is particularly important the first time you have a face-to-face meeting with your child's teacher. That initial conversation sets the tone for all other interactions that will follow, and you want to start off on the right foot.

If you have misgivings—perhaps you are worried about the age of the teacher, or the methods being used to teach reading—keep them to yourself at first. In the course of getting to know the teacher, some of your concerns are likely to vanish. Those that don't can be addressed more constructively when the teacher senses your support and willingness to work side by side with her.

Phrase questions and comments positively. Instead of asking "Why isn't Johnny doing well?" ask "What will help Johnny to do well?" "Why isn't Johnny doing well?" implies that someone or something is at fault, namely the teacher and the school. Right away the teacher becomes defensive and begins explaining what's "wrong" with Johnny—and the conference is off to a bad start.

Asking "What will help Johnny to do well?" is a way of skirting the issue of who is to blame for Johnny's predicament, allowing everyone to focus on what can be done to remedy the problem. When it is framed this way, the question implies a working relationship between school and parent, the kind of relationship from which Johnny will benefit the most.

If you don't understand the terms used by the teacher, ask her to explain. Sometimes teachers use jargon that sounds like complete nonsense to anyone who is not an educator. If you begin to lose your way in a sea of new terms, tell the teacher you don't understand; she will not think less of you if you ask her to explain.

Leave your child at home. Allowing your child to sit in on a conference is counterproductive. It is virtually impossible to discuss anything substantive when your child is in earshot. The teacher will censor her comments and you will not get the sort of information you need or deserve. If you cannot find a baby-sitter, remember that keeping your child occupied will require part of the conference time and you will have less opportunity to visit. If you want to bring your child because you would like to share the teacher's comments with him, leave him at home and share remarks with him when the conference is over.

WHEN TO CHECK IN WITH THE TEACHER

Generally speaking, it is a good idea to check in with your child's teacher at least twice a year for a parent-teacher conference. Most teachers believe twice-a-year conferences are a good idea and schools normally plan fall and spring parent-teacher meetings. (Some schools schedule three parent-teacher conferences each year.) The fall conference lets you know how your child is starting off the school year, the spring conference how your child is finishing out the year. Late afternoons and early evenings are often set aside for conferences for working parents.

Don't feel limited to the twice-a-year conference schedule. Concerns are bound to crop up from time to time over the course of an entire school year. Talk with your child's teacher anytime, especially if something is troubling you. If you are uncertain about when it's important to check in with your child's teacher, do so when you see one of the following things:

If your child consistently brings home unfinished papers or papers with lots of mistakes and corrections, set up a meeting with the teacher. Poor papers may mean that your child has let his classroom work habits slip or that he is having difficulty reading. Both are troublesome and call for a face-to-face meeting with your child's teacher.

If you get a note from the teacher asking your child to complete extra homework papers, pick up the phone and call the school. There is a reason for the teacher's request and your immediate goal should be to find out what that reason is. Phrase your question in such a way that it conveys your willingness to be supportive. You might say something like, "I am calling about the homework you sent home with Johnny. We'll be glad to do all we can to help. Is Johnny having problems with his reading?"

If the teacher answers that Johnny just needs a little extra practice but is doing fine, good. No further contact with the teacher is necessary. But if you get the sense that Johnny is experiencing persistent problems, request a face-to-face meeting. Use the conference to find out what the problem is and then use the learning suggestions in this book as part of the remedy.

If your child tells you that he is in the "low reading group," call his teacher immediately and set up a time for a conference. Being in the low group should be a clear signal to you that your child needs some extra help. Your child may have gotten into, or may be heading for, serious trouble. Under no circumstances should you delay meeting with the teacher. Likewise, if you get a note from the teacher saying your child has been placed in Chapter I reading, call right away. Only poor readers qualify for

Chapter I, the major federally funded program to help children who are having trouble reading. Concern is justified and fast action is required.

Having mentioned several troubling behaviors, a word of caution is in order. Don't depend one hundred percent on your child's rendition of what is happening in his classroom. Sometimes children unknowingly give us less-than-accurate information about school. Messages become garbled or children's perceptions are skewed. When your child tells you about things that go on in school, don't become alarmed until you have had a chance to get additional information from the teacher.

Likewise, given the two-way relationship between home and school, don't be surprised if, from time to time, the teacher hears some strange stories about your family. During my first year of teaching, one of my second-grade girls told me that her high-school-age brother was having difficulty with reading. When I talked with her mother, I learned that the brother was enrolled in a Spanish class and had been practicing reading aloud some of the exercises in his Spanish textbook!

One of the students at the university where I currently work, a fourth-grade teacher who has taught school for many years, tells the parents of the children in her class that she will believe half of the things the children say about them if they will believe only half of the things their children say about her. She is joking, of course, but there *is* some wisdom in what she says.

6

UNDERSTANDING THE
SCHOOL CONNECTION

Gone are the days when every child in a class worked on exactly the same lesson at exactly the same time. The reality of classroom life is this: lots of children are involved in a number of different activities. When children are not reading with the teacher, they might be working on individual assignments, completing projects in small groups, or finding information in reference books.

Gone, too, is the time when every classroom was filled with desks arranged in long, straight rows. Many classrooms, particularly those occupied by kindergarteners and first- and second-graders, don't even have desks—children work at long tables; learning is cooperative. Sometimes furniture isn't used at all, and children sit on the floor. Clearly your child's classroom can be a dynamic place with lots of learning and social interaction.

THE INS AND OUTS
OF READING GROUPS

Some of the interaction that takes place in a classroom comes from the way children gather into small groups for reading instruction. Teachers who use a basal approach typically divide children into three (sometimes more) groups to accommodate high, average, and low-level readers. Flexibility—the teacher's willingness to move children from group to group—is the cardinal rule for successful basal reading groups.

Good teachers will readily move students in and out of groups as their reading abilities change. The child who gets extra help at home and makes better-than-expected progress in school is moved from a low to an average group, or from an average to a high group.

Working with these small groups has a number of advantages. Chief among them is the narrow range of reading abilities that is a greater possibility for small groups than it is for a whole class. A narrower range makes it easier to find materials suited to the children's needs.

This year a friend of mine, Beth, has a third-grade class that she says is typical of those she's had in years past. Of the twenty-seven children in her room, three are reading near the fifth-grade level, five are reading on the fourth-grade level, twelve on the third-grade level, and six are reading on the second-grade level. One child cannot read at all. Obviously, no single book or teaching material is going to meet the needs of every child in this class.

An effective way of handling the wide range of reading abilities typically found in elementary classrooms where basal readers are used is to group children for instruction, as Beth has done with her class. She divided her students into four different reading groups. One group is made up of the eight children who are reading above grade level. The average group—the one reading on grade level—is the largest, with twelve children. The third group is made up of the six children who are reading on the second-grade level. Beth works individually with the one child who cannot read.

Being a good teacher, my friend carefully selects the materials she believes are best suited to the children within each reading group. With reading groups, the range of abilities is narrowed and the reading materials chosen are often a better match for each child's reading level.

With fewer children in a reading group, teachers are able to pay more attention to individual children. This is especially important for shy children and for underachievers. Oftentimes shy children or poorer readers are overlooked when they are part of a large group. Self-confident children with better reading ability who find answers to questions quickly and are enthusiastic about participating in class make it difficult for shy or less-able readers to speak up. Even when teachers help these children adjust to the give-and-take mode of lessons, it isn't easy when better readers are always waiting for a chance to say something. Waiting for shy children or poor readers who may progress less quickly is not something eager, self-confident readers do well, at least not in the early elementary grades, and so shy children and less-able readers must work extra hard just to stay a part of the action.

Equally troubling is the strong tendency of shy and less-able readers to avoid asking questions in large groups. Children are sometimes afraid of looking silly in front of their classmates. Some children are simply too shy to speak out.

I remember a little girl who was so shy that she never raised her hand in class. Whenever the teacher worked with the whole class at once, Janet stared at the papers on her desk. No amount of coaxing could convince Janet to participate. Yet when Janet was placed in a smaller group, a group where she received more individual attention, she would often speak up and join in the lesson. Perhaps Janet felt safer and more confident in a smaller group. Whatever her reason, Janet looked forward to the times when she did not have to compete with the twenty-five other children in her classroom.

Whatever the cause of silence, deciding not to ask questions in class can only slow the learning process further. In the judgment of most teachers, reading is a good time for more personal contact, which is one of the main aims of smaller reading groups.

Reading groups can have drawbacks, however. No child's self-esteem ever profited from being placed in a "low" reading group. It doesn't make a difference whether reading groups are called the Red, Blue, and Green Groups or the Planes, Trains, and Dump Trucks—everyone still knows which group is at the top and which is at the bottom. Children who perceive themselves as the poorest readers in a class don't expect much of themselves when it comes to reading achievement. Likewise, teachers have lower expectations for children in the slow group than for high and average readers.

By watching videotapes of reading lessons in California and Illinois, Collins (66) observed that teachers spent more time teaching comprehension to high-level reading groups and more time teaching phonics to low-level groups. This is due in part to the differences in each child's reading ability. Good readers have solid phonics abilities and reading vocabularies, and are therefore challenged by instruction in comprehension. On the other hand, poor readers are usually weak in the areas of phonics and vocabulary; therefore teachers feel compelled to emphasize these two areas. What is troubling, though, is that poor readers may also be lacking in comprehension, yet may not always be getting much related instruction.

Not only are upper-level groups taught more about comprehension, they learn it at a faster pace than lower-level groups. Given the same amount of time, the high group will do more reading and will progress further in their reading textbooks than children in the low group. As a consequence, we see an ever-widening gap between the best and the poorest readers.

Should high groups continue to progress faster and low groups persist in slower movement, the chances of one group catching up to the other diminishes the longer children stay in school. In many of the sixth-grade classrooms I visit, the poorest students are reading on a first- or second-grade level and the best students are reading on a junior- or senior-high-school level.

As the gap continues to grow, the plight of the poor reader becomes more and more serious. The majority of our poorest readers are destined to eventually leave high school with what amounts to few, if any, useful reading abilities. Reading groups are not the cause of this problem, but a discrepancy in the rate of progress between good and poor readers *is* a contributing factor. A solution might be to use the whole-language approach, in which more of the school day is devoted to reading and writing: to teach reading, writing, and literature several hours each day; to teach only those phonics abilities that are known to be used frequently by readers; to set aside a portion of the school day for reading library books; and to increase the number of opportunities available to students to write and to share their writing with their classmates.

Not all teachers use reading groups. Some prefer to teach the entire class at once. Teachers who like to work this way must reach in the same lesson the least-able reader, who may barely be able to read a few words, and the most accomplished reader, who may be reading several years above grade level. Teaching reading to the whole class at one time is markedly less popular than dividing children into small reading groups. Simultaneously reaching the lowest and the highest readers is too great a stretch to work well in most classrooms, and is nearly impossible in classrooms where basal readers are the backbone of instruction. This no doubt accounts for the less popular view of whole-class reading instruction.

If you want more information about your child's reading group, request a conference with his teacher. Chapter 5, Talking with Your Child's Teacher, offers additional suggestions about what to ask when you get to the conference. If your child is in the low group, have his teacher give you the names of several library books that are suitable for reading at home; use them with the learning activities in the last three chapters of this book.

WHAT TEST SCORES
TELL YOU ABOUT YOUR CHILD

Like reading groups, tests play a fundamental role in the way reading is taught in American schools. Testing is a widely practiced form of evaluation, and it is unlikely that your child will complete the elementary grades without taking at least one, and probably several, reading achievement tests. That you will be given the results of these tests is a certainty.

Most test scores sent home by the school will compare your child's reading ability with that of a group of children who have already taken the test. This "norm group" sets the standard by which your child's reading achievement is judged. To get a sense of how the norm group works, suppose we asked the fifth-graders at Blue Ribbon Elementary School to read a list of words. Looking at the scores, we would probably find a few children who know only a small number of words and a few children who know a great many words. But most of our fifth-grade children would recognize approximately the same number of words.

Now let's suppose that a new fifth-grader moves into town. In order to determine how the new child compares with the other fifth-graders at Blue Ribbon Elementary, we have to find out where the newcomer's word knowledge fits in among the scores already collected. If the new child knows about the same number of words as the majority of the other fifth-graders at Blue Ribbon, we can say that the newcomer has an average level of word knowledge. If the new child knows a great many more words than most fifth-graders, we can say that his vocabulary knowledge is above average. Knowing fewer words indicates that the newcomer's reading vocabulary is below average.

Our fifth-grade group is acting as a norm group—as a kind of yardstick for evaluating reading ability. When you look at your child's reading test results, you are likely to see several different scores that refer to your child's position within a norm group. The scores most often reported to parents are stanines (pronounced "stay-nines"), percentile ranks, and grade equivalents. Of these three scores, stanines are the simplest and are therefore a good place to begin.

Stanines are a nine-point scale, 1 being the lowest, 9 the highest. Stanines 1 through 3 denote below-average achievement, 4 through 6 average ability, and 7 through 9 above-average. Originally called "standard nines," the name stanine comes from this nine-way division of scores.

Stanines were developed during the Second World War when it was a common practice to test the recruits as part of their entry into military service. While widespread testing proved to yield a great deal of information, it also created a storage problem. The perforated cards used to record data at that time had only nine holes in each column, which limited the amount of space available for recording test scores. In order to keep down the number of cards, a decision was made to use one column to record one score. As a consequence, test scores could not exceed the number nine, and the use of stanines was the solution.

Going back to the word-knowledge test we gave to the fifth-graders at Blue Ribbon Elementary, a stanine of 1,

2, or 3 represents below-average knowledge of reading vocabulary (on the low end of our fifth-grade norm group). Stanines of 4, 5, and 6 denote an average level of word knowledge—most children in our fifth-grade norm group fall into this category. Stanines 7, 8, and 9 reflect above-average word knowledge. While stanines have the advantage of being accurate indications of reading ability, they do not provide a detailed picture of precisely where your child stands in comparison to the norm group. More specific information can be found in percentile ranks.

Nearly every reading test in our university reading clinic and nearly every test I work with in the schools reports percentile ranks. Percentile ranks reflect the percentage of children in the norm group who score above and below your child. Depending on where the test publisher begins numbering, percentile ranks range from 0 or 1 (the worst possible performance) all the way to 99+ or 100 (the best performance).

What if your child had a percentile rank of 90 on the word-knowledge test we gave to the fifth-graders at Blue Ribbon? This would mean that your child's vocabulary knowledge is as high as or higher than 90 percent of the fifth-graders we tested. In other words, only 10 percent of the children in our fifth-grade group knew more words than your child. Perhaps the trickiest thing about percentile ranks is remembering how they differ from percentages.

Percentages tell you something about the number right and number wrong—your child knew 75 percent of the words on the test taken by the fifth-graders at Blue Ribbon Elementary. If we had twenty words on our test, 75 percent correct means your child knew fifteen words. Suppose also that only a few children knew as many as 75 percent of the words on our vocabulary test.

In this case, getting 75 percent of the words right would represent a percentile rank of 90—good word knowledge in comparison with the fifth-grade norm group. By letting you know how your child compares with the norm group, percentile ranks translate the number right and the number wrong to a scale that allows you to make a value judgment about performance.

Grade equivalents are different. Written as grade in school plus month, a grade equivalent of 5.5 is read fifth grade–fifth month. Grade equivalents represent the average performance of children in the norm group at a specific time during the school year. Let's assume your child received a grade equivalent of 5.5 on the word-knowledge test we gave to children at Blue Ribbon Elementary.

A grade equivalent of 5.5 means that your child knew the same number of words as the "average" fifth-grader during the month of January. Of course, it would be impossible to give a test every month of every school year to the children in a norm group, so test publishers use statistics to generate average scores when there are gaps in real testing information.

The primary advantage of grade equivalents is their ability to report scores in familiar and easy-to-understand terms—grade in school plus month. Beware! The grade and month numbers can be deceptive. They appear to be giving you more information than they actually do. Given a 5.5 grade equivalent, you assume your child should be doing mid-fifth-grade work and reading halfway through the fifth-grade reader, right? Wrong—both assumptions are flawed.

Unfortunately, grade equivalents do not measure your child's ability to do classroom work, nor do grade equivalents reflect your child's ability to read books written on a certain grade level. One of the reasons that grade equivalents don't offer useful information about classroom reading ability is the discrepancy that often exists between tests and textbooks. Textbooks are written quite differently than reading tests and place greater demands on reading abilities. Textbooks call for reading longer passages, an ability to understand how large groups of facts and ideas are organized, and the skill to interpret visual aids like graphs and charts.

As a rule, grade equivalents overestimate real-life reading capability. Overestimates may be as small as a few months or as large as a few years. The notion that grade equivalents miss the mark is reason enough to be skeptical of these scores. A grade equivalent of twelve, the score we would expect of a high school senior, may correspond to college entrance exam scores that are far too low to qualify for admission to most major universities. The entrance exam scores required by many colleges would be the equivalent of fifteenth grade, which is three years beyond a high school senior's grade in school and corresponds to a junior year in college.

Vocational fields are no different. Students studying electronics or heating–air conditioning systems must read and understand a wide range of technical terms and complex explanations. The biggest problem facing students and their teachers is textbooks that are a struggle to read. Perhaps this happens because the textbooks for vocational students are often written well above students' actual reading level, and well above the reading ability necessary to achieve a grade-equivalent score on the twelfth-grade level.

A third-grader, Yvonne, stands out in my memory as one of the many cases in which grade equivalents have been misleading. When Yvonne came to our university reading clinic, she brought with her copies of the reading achievement test given by her school. In looking over reading grade equivalents, it seemed as though Yvonne was making slightly below average progress. She had a grade equivalent of 2.5 which, while it was below her actual third-grade status in school, wasn't a disturbing score. When I asked her mother the reason for Yvonne's referral to our clinic, I discovered that Yvonne's classroom teacher thought that Yvonne needed lots of extra help. The teacher was right. We found that Yvonne could barely read a preprimer, the easiest book used in first grade. She did have a serious reading problem, but it had not shown up in her grade-equivalent scores.

If grade equivalents were reliable indicators of real-life reading ability, a grade equivalent of 2.5 should be high enough to correspond to second-grade reading ability. My recommendation to parents is to look at grade equivalents with a cautious eye—many test publishers are phasing them out primarily because the score is so difficult to interpret with certainty.

Given that your child's school will send home stanines, percentile ranks, and (maybe) grade equivalents, how can you go about interpreting these scores? As an example, let's see what a sample set of scores says about reading strengths and weaknesses. We'll assume your child's second-grade teacher sent home the following scores from an achievement test:

	Stanine	Percentile Rank	Grade Equivalent
Reading Comprehension	4	38	2.3
Vocabulary	8	91	3.2
Phonics	7	80	2.9
Total Reading	6	64	2.6

The way your child scored on the entire test is reported on the line labeled "Total Reading." Each of the other three areas—comprehension, vocabulary, and phonics—is a subtest of the larger test.

The first conclusion we can draw is that your child's overall reading ability falls within an average range. A Total Reading percentile rank of 6 places your child near the top of the "average" group—stanines 4, 5, and 6 represent average performance. Because three separate scores are folded into the Total Reading score, it is potentially misleading. If your child's scores are particularly strong on a few subtests, they may overshadow a weakness you need to know about.

Comparing one subtest to another gives you a clearer picture of your child's reading strengths and weaknesses. Say your child is particularly strong in vocabulary and phonics, but less solid in comprehension. A percentile rank of 8 in vocabulary and 7 in phonics clearly places your child in the above-average group in these two areas. Your child correctly answered more vocabulary questions than 91 percent of the children in the norm group and more phonics questions than 80 percent of the norm group.

When compared to his strong ability in vocabulary and phonics, your child's ability to comprehend what he reads is much less well-developed. While a percentile rank of 4 stands for average performance, it is the lowest percentile rank in that range. Your child correctly answered more comprehension questions than only 38 percent of the norm group. At the time the test was taken, your child's comprehension wasn't low enough to be considered an area of weakness, but the comprehension score is obviously out of line with that of vocabulary and phonics. Such discrepancies are troubling and should not be overlooked.

I would interpret this difference as an early warning that problems may be brewing. If your child's comprehension continues to slip, he eventually will be able to pronounce the words in storybooks, but will be unable to understand the meaning of the sentences. The wisest course of action at this point is to set up a conference with your child's teacher. Explain your concerns and get some suggestions of good books your child can read at home.

Given the sample set of scores, it is early enough for a bit of extra effort to go a long way. If you turn to Chapter 12, Comprehension Learning Activities, you'll find a number of comprehension learning activities described. With the practice that comes from reading library books for pleasure, and with extra help at home and at school, your child's comprehension will soon improve and a potentially serious reading problem will never have the chance to develop.

Perhaps you've noticed that I haven't mentioned grade-equivalent scores, even though they were reported. Again, because grade equivalents have the potential to give an inaccurate picture of your child's actual reading ability, they do not offer much insight into reading strengths and weaknesses. For this reason, it is safer to rely on stanines and percentile ranks. If you want to know at which level your child is reading, ask the teacher what grade-level book he is reading in class. (You'll recall this is my first question on the list in Chapter 5.)

THE SOCIAL SIDE OF LEARNING

Above all else, classrooms are social settings. Learning to read, and learning in other subject-matter areas, depends on your child's ability to cope constructively with his classroom's social climate. This ability requires a certain amount of self-control and social skill.

In the years I've been teaching, I have never seen a poorly behaved classroom of youngsters who learned very much. Children who don't know how to control their behavior lose valuable instructional time, do not complete their work, and generally suffer from underachievement.

Amid all the activity in a normal classroom, the social graces have an important place. Children who bring to school pleasant social behavior and habits, and the ability to focus their attention on assignments, learn a great deal more than those who come without these skills. At the risk of seeming a bit old-fashioned, I've noticed that many of the children I work with could benefit from lessons in how to behave politely and pleasantly. "Thank you," "You're welcome," "Please," and "Excuse me" could stand more widespread use.

Similarly, when working in school, children need to sit still and to concentrate on the learning task at hand—no leg-swinging, rocking backward in the chair, continuous dropping and picking up paper and pencils. They should also avoid talking too much to neighbors and develop the ability to stick with a task until it is finished.

Given the social climate of classrooms today, paying attention is vital. Marty, a friend who teaches Spanish in an elementary school, says that paying attention makes a difference in the kind of Spanish words the children in her class learn. When she can, Marty uses Spanish to talk with the children in her classroom. While most of the children are learning things like "That's a nice new shirt you have on today" or "When is Clarissa's birthday?" a few are learning phrases like "Sit down," "Put your feet on the floor, not the desk," and "Don't hit."

The difference, Marty says, is that a couple of children do not pay attention, regardless of what the rest of the class is doing. They don't pay attention when other children are using Spanish words in class, and so they miss out on a great deal of learning. Needless to say, inattentive children do not make the same kind of progress as those who listen and participate do.

Along with social amenities there must come an understanding that physical violence (hitting, kicking, pushing) is not permitted, that talking is the better, more reasonable way to solve differences. From my perspective, the art of working cooperatively could benefit from a bit more cultivation. There is, of course, a fine line between suppressing a child's natural curiosity and spirit, and asking for cooperative classroom behavior. By insisting that children need to pay attention and exercise restraint, I am not suggesting that we put our children in social straitjackets. What is needed is a balance between courteous, attentive behavior and spirited, spontaneous behavior.

7

RECOGNIZING TROUBLE
BEFORE IT'S TOO LATE

The idea that all children should grow up to be literate is somewhat new to American society. One hundred and fifty years ago, relatively few people could read because skilled reading wasn't as essential for getting along in society. One hundred years ago a person was thought to be literate if he could write his name.

It wasn't until this century that the level of reading ability required for one to live comfortably within modern society increased in any significant way. Persons born just after the turn of the century were thought of as educated if they had attended elementary school and acquired rudimentary reading ability. A reading ability that was suitable in the workplace of fifty years ago is not sufficient to enter into and succeed in today's high-tech job market.

We have every reason to believe that the standard for literacy will continue to rise, and at a faster pace than in years past. Increasingly high standards are certain to affect today's elementary schoolchildren more than any other generation of Americans. At the beginning of the twenty-first century, the standard for functional literacy—the minimal reading ability required to make a living—will be well beyond the level needed for success in today's job market.

Seniors leaving high school this year with only minimal reading ability will fall below the standard for functional literacy long before their working careers are over. Rising standards are certain to have serious economic repercussions since a great many workers will have to either drop out of the labor force or seek further reading instruction to hold their jobs.

THE DROPOUT SYNDROME

The chances are good that your child will read far above any standard for functional literacy, but the impact of rising standards must be taken into account when we think about how the American educational process is being restructured. Not too long ago, children whose reading ability lagged behind that of their classmates had some chance of catching up in junior and senior high school. This situation is changing rapidly.

The concern regarding our nation's lack of competitiveness in world markets has led to a call for more rigorous and productive educational programs. Former Secretary of Education William J. Bennett (67), in his much-talked-about James Madison High School model, suggested that American high school students be required to take four years of English; three years each of social studies, mathematics, and science; two years each of a foreign language and physical education; and one half of a year each of art and music.

Whether or not Secretary Bennett's recommendations are adopted in your school district, the idea of introducing substantive improvements in American education has been embraced nationwide by school boards, principals, teachers, and parents. Upgrading American education means that a high school student's chance of making up for poor reading achievement and at the same time doing well in other rigorous subject matter courses is slim at best, maybe nonexistent.

With less flexibility to catch u₋, children who fall behind in reading during the elementary years enter high school with a high risk of failing courses and becoming dropouts. According to a recent government report (68), in 1985 there were approximately 4.3 million dropouts between the ages of sixteen and twenty-four. When asked about school, dropouts reported they didn't like their classes. It's no wonder—these young people were failing high school courses, did not have the reading ability to understand their textbooks, and were struggling with the same assignments their classmates completed with ease.

The majority of dropouts find themselves among the ranks of the unemployed who are not able to find any sort of work at all. Dropouts who *are* fortunate enough to find work end up in less desirable jobs because they are the only positions that do not require a reasonable level of reading ability.

Anchored in the nature of childhood experiences, the value parents place on the importance of a good education, the quality of schools attended, and many other factors, illiteracy has no single cause. It is clear, however, that children who fail to climb the reading pyramid, who get behind and then do not climb high enough or fast enough, leave high school unequipped to earn a living. While we cannot pinpoint with certainty the causes of illiteracy, it is easy to forecast its onset.

Each year there are approximately 200,000 nine-year-olds who cannot read (69). Two hundred thousand children per year is a staggering number, but more alarming perhaps is what this number portends for the future. Nine-year-old children should be making the transition from the lower tiers of the reading pyramid (the primary grades) to upper tiers (the upper grades). These children have already spent three and one-half years in school, yet they are at the bottom of the reading pyramid unable to read even simple books.

There is no question that the 200,000 nine-year-old children sitting in today's classrooms, unable to read their textbooks and faced with assignments they cannot possibly complete, are tomorrow's illiterates. What will happen to these nine-year-olds at the end of elementary school? Forty percent of thirteen-year-olds in American schools cannot read well enough to understand their textbooks (69). These youngsters cannot possibly be expected to gain much, if anything, from school. In addition to developing a strong dislike of school and a tendency to drop out, many less skilled readers cause tremendous problems for their teachers. Behavior problems are so serious that, in some schools, drastic action is necessary. One New Jersey principal resorted to carrying a baseball bat around his school!

Certainly not all behavior problems are tied to reading failure, but many serious incidences of misconduct have found their roots in school failure. The link between reading disability and disruptive behavior is certainly strong enough that it is worth exploring further.

READING FAILURE OR MISCONDUCT: WHICH COMES FIRST?

When we reflect on the causes of a child's reading disability we are looking back in time. It is difficult, sometimes impossible, to be absolutely certain of what has contributed to a child's reading problems and what is an outgrowth of school failure. The causes and consequences of reading failure are often intertwined when we look into the past.

Perhaps the most important thing to remember is this:

the connection between reading failure and behavior problems can go either way. Some children begin school with an emotional chip on their shoulders, others do not. I can remember sitting in a principal's office, listening to one child walk down the hall banging on the walls and shouting unpleasant things as she went. When I asked the principal about the reasons for the disturbance, he explained that the child was no longer living at home due to the level of violence that existed in the family's day-to-day life.

This little girl brought to kindergarten these strong feelings of hostility—no wonder she was aggressive, argumentative, and inconsiderate of the other children's property. Both the school and social services were working with her. This same little girl was a poor reader. Even if I could have given her a magic potion to improve her reading, her emotional problems would have remained. In fact, the emotional problems she brought with her to school contributed significantly to her reading difficulty. In this instance, emotional problems were largely responsible for her reading failure, but there are far more children for whom the connection between reading failure and disruptive behavior works in the opposite direction—failure in school comes first, followed by behavior problems.

By fourth grade, Evan had established a reputation as being one of the most difficult children in his school. Everyone tried to shape his disruptive behavior to fit a more congenial mold, but nothing worked. Evan was one of the poorest readers in his class; he was also one of the brightest children, but no one would ever have guessed it.

As Evan watched his classmates read books and complete assignments he struggled with, he began to feel more and more alienated from them and from his teacher. One way children like Evan pretend to cope with failure is by adopting an "I don't care" attitude to cover up despair. A child who doesn't care about doing well doesn't lose self-esteem when he fails. These children are unwilling or unable to express their deep concern about the situations they find themselves in. The little boy, Pierre, in Maurice Sendak's *Really Rosie* (48) is a good example of this kind of child—Pierre changes his "I don't care" mind set for a positive, caring attitude. The moral here is that caring is an essential part of living, and that all children care about the people and events in their lives, no matter how much they might have you believe otherwise.

If I could have given Evan a magic potion to improve his reading, we probably would have seen his classroom behavior improve. In the fourth grade Evan did get a magic potion of sorts—he entered a special reading program. This program concentrated one hundred percent on reading, math, and building a healthy self-image. As Evan's reading ability improved so did his classroom behavior. Eventually, Evan began to feel comfortable with his textbooks and to make an effort to participate in a normal classroom routine. By the time he was ready for junior high school, Evan was reading on grade level. He was also a bright, eager learner, something no one would have predicted.

No one wishes for this kind of uphill struggle for their children. Schooling takes a long time and requires a great deal of effort. There are many, many places where things can and do go wrong, and none of us want to find out too late that our child is in serious trouble.

On the other hand, the normal ups and downs of learning will always be a part of your child's school experiences. Knowing this, it's important to separate healthy, natural concerns (those things that you might worry about but probably shouldn't) from real signs of trouble (things you need to worry about).

WHOLESOME CONCERNS

Some reading habits are signs of trouble, others are not. Because it's difficult to know when to worry and when not to worry, it becomes easy to get caught up in a stressful cycle of worry and concern. As your child goes through the elementary grades you are likely to wonder about one, if not all, of the four behaviors described here. Each is a wholesome concern, not worth losing sleep over but worth noting.

My child only reads "easy" books. At one time or another most children are attracted to books that are really too easy for their reading ability. Suppose your third-grader brings home library books best suited to children reading on a second-grade level. This worries you because it seems logical that if your child only reads easy books his reading ability will never improve. Technically your logic works, but in reality very different factors come into play.

Remember your child will be reading more challenging books at school; the teacher will see to it that classroom reading experiences will help students continue to climb up the reading pyramid. What's more, there are sizable benefits to be gained from reading simple books. Reading the same words over and over again leads to faster word recognition. Rapid word identification gives your child more time to pay attention to meaning, allowing comprehension to improve—a benefit that remains when your child switches to harder books.

Improved fluency, characterized by smooth, fluid, effortless reading, is another advantage of reading easy books. Because your child knows all the words in simple books, full attention can be focused on capturing the tone and rhythm of the different kinds of sentences.

Reading easy books is a confidence builder, too. There is no better way to build self-esteem than by reading books fluently and without help from anyone. The more easy books your child reads, the more his self-esteem is bound to grow. Eventually your child will want to return to reading harder books, but in the meantime he will gain from the experiences of reading easy books.

My child doesn't read as much as I did when I was young. We are likely to judge our children's reading habits by standards carried over from our own childhood experiences. If we were avid readers as children, we tend to expect that our children will be avid readers as well. If we were the kinds of kids who spent more time outdoors or in front of the television set than we did reading books, our yardstick for judging recreational reading includes fewer books.

"My sixth-grade son Mark doesn't read nearly enough," Mark's mother confided in me after a meeting at his school last fall. "How much does Mark routinely read?" I asked. "Two or three nights a week, he spends a short time reading before he goes to sleep. But that's not nearly as much as I read when I was his age," was her reply. As it turned out, Mark spent the majority of his free time pursuing sports, watching television, and sharpening his video-game skills. This behavior troubled his mother.

That Mark was falling short of his mother's expectations for his leisure reading is clear. It is also clear that Mark was spending a lot more time reading for pleasure than most children his age. Perhaps what Mark's mother found most troubling was that reading did not head up Mark's list of favorite activities. This isn't unusual, though. When I explained that it's normal for children who enjoy leisure reading to say that they prefer activities like sports and being with friends, Mark's mother relaxed.

We want our children to be avid readers, but demanding that they spend more time reading is likely to have the opposite effect. If your child, like Mark, spends some of his leisure time reading but prefers other activities, stop worrying for a while. Perhaps the best way to interest your child in recreational reading is to find those books suited to your child's interests and read them together, one chapter a night or whatever amount fits your life-style. The most probable outcome is that he'll find himself captivated by the book and will eventually, without pressure from you, look for another book in the series or another book by the same author. Rely on reading aloud, on the book-sharing ideas mentioned in Chapter 3, and, if you think it might be helpful, on some of the reading spark plugs from Chapter 1.

My child's reading interests are too narrow. Sarah, the third-grader who lives across the street, reads books about horses, nothing else. She spends her weekends riding, the walls in her bedroom are covered with horse pictures, and her bookshelves are filled with books and magazines about horses. If you are an avid reader yourself, you are going to feel uneasy if your child limits reading to one topic or genre, be it mysteries, Westerns, or science fiction. But don't worry: children typically go through phases when they read a steady diet of the same kind of book or books, on the same topic. As long as your child is reading, let him explore the same subject or the same literary form until the need to read different kinds of books reappears. The elementary school reading program will introduce your child to books, poems, and plays written on a variety of different topics. Sooner or later your child's reading interests will widen, but in the meantime he'll exhaust the topic or literary form he has chosen.

My child doesn't want to read on his own. He would rather have me read aloud to him. If your child is doing well in school, don't worry if he prefers listening to stories read aloud to reading books on his own. *Do* continue reading aloud, but take it one step further: ask your child to read along with you. Find an interesting book on an easy level and ask your child to join you as you read. Read at a comfortable pace, holding a marker under each line if your child needs help keeping his place. When you come to a word your child is unsure of, let your voice move slightly ahead so your child can hear you say the word correctly.

This simple technique has been used for many years as a means of improving reading fluency. Improved fluency—the kind of smooth oral reading we associate with skilled readers—comes when your child imitates your good oral reading habits. This method incorporates the benefits of reading aloud while at the same time offering your child a chance to share reading time with you—a perfect combination!

WARNING SIGNS:
WHEN IT'S WORTH WORRYING

All too often minor difficulties go unnoticed. But little problems have a way of turning into big problems, and before long a serious reading disability has arisen. By knowing what to look for, taking action quickly, and working in harmony with your child's teacher, you can often avoid reading problems and contribute immeasurably to your child's overall success in school.

Just as signs along the highway alert drivers to upcoming dangerous curves, construction, or slippery pavement, reading warning signs tell us something is amiss. Children who habitually show warning signs need immediate help!

Before going further I would like to put warning signs into perspective. From time to time you are bound to observe one or more of these warning signs. Seeing a warning sign every now and then is not necessarily a problem; you are probably only observing the normal ups and downs of the learning-to-read process. Only when you begin to notice your child routinely showing a warning sign should you be concerned.

My child "reads" the pictures in his books, not the words. Because pictures help to explain a story, less skilled readers often use them as a substitute for reading the text. Some children weave whole stories around pictures. When these children open a book, they try immediately to interpret the message using the pictures rather than the print. The simplest explanation for overdependence on pictures to tell a story is that the book is too hard.

Difficult books contain a great many words your child cannot recognize, so he uses the pictures as clues to information. If you suspect this is happening, ask your child's teacher to recommend a few books she believes might be a good match for your child's reading ability. If your child's behavior changes and he begins to pay attention to the words in the books his teacher recommends, the solution is straightforward: make certain your child reads books that are not too difficult.

If reading easier books does not unglue your child from pictures, you have a reason to worry. Being dependent on pictures means that your child's reading vocabulary may be severely underdeveloped. If so, your child needs to learn more words immediately. Contact the teacher about helping your child to build a solid reading vocabulary using the phonics and vocabulary activities found in Chapters 10 and 11 of this book.

Having identified overemphasis/dependence on pictures as a warning sign, I would like to point out that it *is* important for children to enjoy the beautiful, expressive illustrations that are an integral part of many children's books, especially the books read by younger elementary-age children. As a first-grader, Marla relished the lively pictures in the books that she read, and she always looked at the pictures in her books before she read the words. Now that Marla is in the fourth grade, the books that she reads have few, if any, illustrations. Once, when Marla was reading James Howe's book *Morgan's Zoo* (49)—a delightful story about the efforts of two children and a collection of animals with human qualities to keep a zoo open—she told me that she didn't miss seeing pictures on every page but preferred to create her own pictures in her mind.

Although children eventually come to rely on the words in books to create their own mental images of the stories they read, illustrations are a delightful, enriching source of pleasure for children and adults. We want our children to learn to enjoy illustrations; we do not want our children to use them as substitutes for reading the words in their books.

My child does a lot of wild guessing. Sometimes children try to compensate for a weak reading vocabulary by making wild guesses, guesses that don't resemble unknown words in meaning or in sound. If your child misses a lot of words, call the teacher at once. It is possible that your child is bringing home library books that are more difficult to read than his ability permits.

On the other hand, missing a large number of words can also be a sign that your child's ability to use phonics is underdeveloped and his overall reading vocabulary is lagging behind. If this is the case, use the learning suggestions in Chapter 10, Phonics Learning Activities, and Chapter 11, Vocabulary Learning Activities. Once your child develops good phonics ability and his reading vocabulary increases, he will give up wild guessing in favor of using phonics and sentence meaning to read correctly the words in his storybooks.

My fourth-, fifth-, or sixth-grader reads everything out loud. There are times when oral reading is appropriate—reading for an audience, reading poetry, sharing an excerpt from an interesting newspaper article, etc. For the most part, however, silent reading is much more efficient than reading aloud. Pronouncing every word, whether audibly or mumbled under one's breath, takes a lot of time. This kind of oral reading limits speed significantly and frequently interferes with comprehension.

By the time a child is standing on the upper tiers of the reading pyramid, silent reading is the predominant mode. Only when faced with extraordinarily difficult material should your fourth-, fifth-, or sixth-grader resort to oral reading. A preference for reading aloud is almost always a clear sign of trouble. If you are not sure whether your child is reading silently or orally, find a passage your child hasn't read in his social studies textbook (or any other subject matter text he uses in school). Hand him the book and say, "Here are two pages in your social studies book. Please read these pages silently to yourself."

Watch what your child does when he reads those pages. Does your child move his lips, nod his head, or mumble to himself? If he does, your child is reading orally rather than silently. Call the teacher. Work as a partner with the school, using the vocabulary and comprehension activities in Chapters 11 and 12 to help your child at home.

My child knows all the words but doesn't understand what he reads. This problem arises when children have spent too much classroom time on phonics drills and not enough time on comprehension. When classroom instruction places a heavy emphasis on learning phonics principles, children may get the impression that all they need to do is say the right words—that comprehension doesn't count. These children think good reading is good "word calling."

Listening to these children read is impressive. Good "word callers" read with remarkable fluency, but with a fluency that is superficial—while they sound like excellent readers, they remember very little of what they read. This is a serious problem that will not go away without extra help. If your child has no difficulty recognizing words but cannot remember what he reads, use the activities in Chapter 12, Comprehension Learning Activities, in combination with a solid program of extra help at school.

My child reads very slowly. He stops at almost every word. In *Becoming a Nation of Readers* (60), the Commission on Reading describes children who put so much emphasis on figuring out the pronunciation of each word that comprehension falls short. A sentence read aloud sounds like this: "The—little—dog—ran—away—from—the—truck." Because these children pause at every word, they are called "word-by-word readers."

Slow, labored, word-by-word reading is a warning sign that children are off-track. Children who read slowly, stopping at nearly every word, need immediate assistance. These children need to increase the number of words they recognize on sight, and to develop better comprehension, and they need to gain good reading fluency.

If your child reads this way, concentrate on Chapters 11 and 12. Work on improving your child's reading fluency by checking out books from the public library that contain words your child already knows and by using the read-aloud suggestion listed under the fourth wholesome concern in this chapter. Your child's teacher has probably noticed the problem, and a short conversation will help the two of you to coordinate efforts.

RULES OF THUMB
FOR GETTING EXTRA HELP

Once you suspect your child may be falling behind, the first question you need to ask yourself is if you should push for a lot of extra help at school. This is a crucial question. Unnecessary action is costly and time-consuming; delaying necessary help is a mistake we'd all like to avoid. To make the decision easier, I have included a few reliable rules of thumb to help you decide whether or not your child really does need special help. Different rules apply to children in different stages of the elementary school reading program, so let's begin with kindergartners.

At the minimum, children finishing kindergarten should know the names of the letters of the alphabet and how to write them, the sounds associated with some or all of the letters, how to write their own names, and how to recognize several words on sight. This knowledge guarantees that children will benefit from a first-grade program. If your child enters first grade unable to do these things, expect a slow start.

Many schools prefer to send all or most of their kindergartners to first grade in the hope that they will improve sometime during that first-grade year. Many children do. It isn't imperative that you take immediate action, but you do need to be particularly watchful throughout your child's first-grade year. Keep in close touch with the teacher and be prepared to give your child lots of support at home.

On the other hand, immediate action may be necessary in situations in which children have been unable to cope with the day-to-day activities in their kindergarten classrooms and have fallen behind their classmates in their knowledge of the alphabet, numbers, colors, etc. These children are in double jeopardy: they lack the basic knowledge that is important for success in the first grade, and their poor social adjustment results in inappropriate classroom behavior. Upon entering first grade, many of these children may not be able to follow the directions given by their teachers, complete classroom activities, or develop healthy relationships with their classmates.

When Mickey entered kindergarten he was the most immature child in his classroom. His attention span was shorter than that of the other children; he cried easily, had few playmates, and preferred to spend all of his time building with the wooden blocks his teacher provided and painting pictures. Mickey's teacher provided him with a variety of classroom activities that were suitable for his abilities, but still, at the end of the school year, Mickey was far behind his kindergarten classmates. He couldn't write his name, count to ten, or name the letters of the alphabet. Some elementary schools have a "transition" level—classrooms that include some kindergarten and some first-grade activities—for children like Mickey who might benefit from an additional year of schooling before entering first grade. Other schools have policies that permit children to be retained in kindergarten for an additional school year. Still others place these children in first grade, but provide educational programs that offer plenty of extra help to children.

Teachers are sensitive to children's progress in kindergarten because they know that the real crunch will come when children are in the first, second, and third grades. The rule of thumb here for getting substantial extra help is a six-month delay in reading achievement. This means that children who are half a year or more behind their classmates are in serious trouble. On the surface, six months doesn't seem like much of a gap. It isn't even a whole school year, you think, so why be concerned?

The answer hinges on the action-packed primary reading program, which covers a great deal of educational ground. Children can't afford to get far behind with such a busy program—there is simply too much catching up to do. As a consequence, even a six-month lag is a critical one.

Intervention must be aggressive and it must be immediate. Get extra help through ongoing school programs and work with your child at home. Do not delay—a child who is six months behind in the primary grades is at risk for experiencing reading difficulty for many years to come.

How about children in the upper grades—fourth, fifth, sixth? What is the rule here? I suggest you seek extra help if your child is reading one year below grade level. A fifth-grade child reading in a fourth-grade book will not catch up on his own. Ask the teacher if you are unsure of your child's reading level. The earlier you intervene, the sooner your child will be climbing the reading pyramid alongside his classmates.

There is one more rule of thumb—the double-time rule. For every month a child falls behind in reading, that child must work double time to make up for the loss. Consider the child beginning third grade who has completed only half of the second-grade reading program. What happens in the third grade? He cannot begin in the third-grade book, so he begins third grade by finishing the last part of the second-grade curriculum. Now that child must make one and one-half years of progress during the third grade just to be an average reader by the time he enters fourth grade. The double-time rule emphasizes the importance of keeping to a minimum the amount of catching up that a child must do.

8

CAN YOUR CHILD
GET DYSLEXIA?

Some children have normal childhoods up until the time they enter school. Then something abnormal happens—instead of learning to read like the other children in their classes, they begin to have problems. Even with good instruction, loving parents, and reports of excellent health, these children have great difficulty learning to read. *Dyslexia* is the term often used to describe this reading disorder.

The word "dyslexia" is a combination of the roots "dys," meaning bad, difficult, or abnormal, and "lexia," which refers to print. Briefly, dyslexia is characterized by an abnormal method of dealing with written symbols, particularly letters and words. Another term used to describe severe reading problems is "learning disability." Learning disability has the same connotations as dyslexia, but encompasses difficulties in mathematics as well. Teachers usually refer to children who have severe reading problems as learning disabled, while physicians and research psychologists tend to call these children dyslexic.

Whether we use the term dyslexic or learning disabled, the presence of either is puzzling in children who should be good readers. These children are intelligent and healthy, have normal vision and hearing, and attend good schools. But instead of learning to read at the standard pace, dyslexic children make extremely slow progress, and some children do not progress at all.

We know dyslexic children have great difficulty remembering and making sense out of the words in their storybooks, but we do not know exactly what causes the problem. Ask ten experts to name the causes of dyslexia and you'll get ten different answers. More than any other learning difficulty, dyslexia continues to puzzle researchers, physicians, teachers, and parents.

Dyslexia is not something children "catch" like the flu. It cannot be transmitted from one child to another because it is not a disease. If dyslexia were contagious, like mumps or chicken pox, it would be more easily dealt with—researchers would conduct experiments to find the responsible organism. Once located, a vaccine could be developed to prevent—maybe even cure—the disorder. Unlike a communicable disease, however, dyslexia is a preexisting condition, something that children are born with or that arises from a serious head injury.

Recent evidence has led researchers to believe that the brains of children and adults with severe reading disorders differ from those of normal readers. Still, the exact ways in which brains differ are unknown since dyslexic children do not exhibit the signs that physicians use to diagnose brain dysfunction, such as paralysis or cerebral bleeding. Instead, these children exhibit "soft signs" of neurological disorders, signs like delayed language learning, distractability, difficulty understanding spoken requests, problems telling left from right, and poor hand-eye coordination. While the presence of these soft signs does suggest brain dysfunction, these signs do not provide conclusive evidence for specific types of brain differences.

Because we cannot put a finger on this disorder, parents are bombarded with misleading, and sometimes completely inaccurate, information. If you want to learn more about recent developments in research and teaching, I suggest writing to the Orton Dyslexia Society, 724 York Road, Baltimore, Maryland 21204. This group of researchers, teachers, and parents is interested in learning more about the nature of dyslexia and about the best ways to teach learning-disabled children. The Orton Dyslexia Society publishes a newsletter called *Perspectives on Dyslexia,* an annual collection of research articles entitled *Annals of Dyslexia,* and an assortment of helpful pamphlets and monographs. If you would like general information about dyslexia, ask for the packet of materials available from this society.

CHILDREN WITH DYSLEXIA

Dyslexia is a complex and perplexing condition. It often doesn't show up in children until they go to school since it is specifically related to the kinds of learning the schools expect. Unlike diseases that have specific sets of symptoms, dyslexia takes many forms. In kindergarten, children may have difficulty remembering the names of the letters, learning to read the words for colors, following directions, and paying attention or carrying out activities that require good hand-eye coordination like coloring, drawing, and writing alphabet letters. As first-graders, dyslexic children may exhibit a variety of problems—severely limited reading vocabularies, poor spelling, inability to comprehend stories, or illegible handwriting.

One of the reasons dyslexia has so perplexed teachers and parents is that dyslexic children exhibit different combinations of disabilities. However, there are seven characteristics that are frequently observed in dyslexic children. Over the years, I've worked with children who have displayed all of the characteristics and children who exhibited only a few. Still, all of the dyslexic children I have taught had severe discrepancies between their intellectual abilities and their reading achievement.

Problems perceiving print. As early as 1925, Samuel Orton, a professor of psychology and a pioneer in the study of dyslexia for whom the Orton Dyslexia Society is named, observed that children who perceived letters backwards, reversed, or upside down exhibited severe reading problems. Orton used the term *strephosymbolia* (meaning mixed symbols) to describe the condition. The presence of severe visual perceptual problems is obvious even to the casual observer. When children perceive words backwards and write words backwards, it is clear that they are processing print differently from normal readers. Yet not all dyslexic children exhibit such dramatic and easily recognized characteristics.

Inability to remember written words. Dyslexic children have a great deal of trouble remembering words from one day to the next and often struggle with the same words their classmates have learned with ease. However, the exact nature of memory disorders in children is unclear. Some researchers speculate that these children do not use effective learning strategies; others believe that their ability to recall mental images of words is impaired. Whatever the cause of the memory deficits in these children, we know that giving dyslexic children more practice seeing and saying words isn't enough.

They need instruction beyond that found in typical classroom teaching methods, learning that involves all the senses—seeing, hearing, tracing, and feeling the shapes of the letters in words. When fourth-grade Gearheart came to our university reading clinic, we used a multisensory teaching method to help him to form mental images of words. We put approximately a half-inch of salt in the bottom of a shallow container. Then we asked Gearheart to look at words written on three-by-five-inch cards, to write the words in the salt, and to say the letters as he wrote them. When he made mistakes, as he often did, Gearheart erased his errors by gently shaking the container. As a dyslexic child's reading vocabulary increases, it is often possible to phase out the use of time-consuming multi-sensory approaches in favor of quicker, more traditional classroom teaching methods.

Difficulty using phonics. When asked, most dyslexic children can tell you beginning letter-sounds—the sound for the letter **s** in **sail,** or the sound for the letter **a** in **ate.** Once beyond the first letter-sound combination, however, many dyslexic children run into difficulty. These children are unable to go systematically from the beginning letter-sound combination in a word to that at the end. As a consequence, many children know the first sound but must guess at the rest of the word, an inefficient and error-filled strategy. Seeing the word **sail** in a storybook, a learning-disabled child may offer guesses like **silver** or **soda.**

A major reason for this difficulty with phonics stems from dyslexics' inability to recognize sounds as the building blocks of words. In order to make sense of phonics, children need to understand that words are divided into parts (like the three sounds in **sit** that go with the three letters **s, i, t**). What's more, they must be able to blend these separate sounds together to produce a recognizable word.

Several years ago, a coworker and I asked first-graders to separate spoken words into sounds. The children who did not know that words like **may** have two distinct sounds were not reading. On the other hand, the children who were making average reading progress were quite skilled at finding sounds in words. As much as three years later, the children who began first grade with a vague notion that words are built of sounds were still having great difficulties reading.

Poor spelling. Extremely poor spelling and severe reading disabilities often go hand in hand. Elena Boder (70) describes three groups of poor spellers. First, there are children who have poor memories for words, like Gearheart. Because these children are forced to rely on phonics when they spell, they use the right sounds and the wrong letters—they might write **bic,** having intended to spell **bike.** The second group of poor spellers is unable to use phonics, and must therefore rely completely on memory. The words they misspell have few correct letter-sound relationships. For example, a child in this group might write **bepe** for **bike.** When they have a mixture of problems—poor memories for words and poor phonics—these children misspell nearly all the words they write. Their mistakes bear no resemblance to the words they are trying to spell, and so it is impossible to decipher the words they write. A child in this category might just as well write **rov** when trying to spell **bike.**

It is important to remember that good and poor readers alike misspell words. Some words in the English language are notoriously difficult to spell—they are the "spelling demons" and are frequently misspelled by children and adults. Consequently, the presence of spelling errors probably doesn't mean that your child is dyslexic. However, if your child is unable to read, or is making very slow progress, and is also an extremely poor speller, it is worth asking the school to look closely at his abilities.

Poor hand-eye coordination. Children with poor hand-eye coordination have illegible handwriting, draw poorly, exhibit difficulty coloring within the lines, and have problems controlling small implements like scissors. Even with a great deal of effort, these children are unable to produce neat, legible handwriting like other children in their classrooms. Still, poor handwriting need not be cause for alarm, nor should the persistent use of manuscript, the block-style letters children learn to write in the early grades, be considered a sign signaling the presence of dyslexia. Certain children find manuscript, with its straight lines and disconnected letters, easier to write than cursive, the system most adults use. It is the presence of poor hand-eye coordination, a soft sign of neurological dysfunction, along with severe reading disabilities, that distinguishes dyslexic children from normal children who have poor penmanship.

Difficulties with comprehension. Another characteristic exhibited by certain dyslexic children is a difficulty understanding the meaning of the stories in their reading books. These children do not completely understand the plot, forget details, change the order of events, and lose track of characters. One of the reasons that dyslexic children have difficulties with reading comprehension is this: they put a tremendous amount of effort into identifying written words. With so much attention going into word recognition, dyslexic children have little time left for comprehension. Consequently, these children have trouble making sense of the sentences in their books.

To add to the problem, dyslexic children seem to be relatively unaware of their own reading mistakes. When good readers make mistakes, they correct themselves, especially if the mistake changes the meaning of what is being read. This is not so with many learning-disabled readers. Dyslexic children tend to overlook mistakes and go on, even when the mistakes change the meaning of what they're reading.

Many researchers believe that problems with reading

comprehension are manifestations of basic disabilities that result from the means dyslexic children use to process spoken language. In part, difficulties with spoken language are believed to arise from impaired abilities to reason and use symbols. When dyslexic children are asked to make sense of written sentences, their difficulties with language are instantly compounded because printed symbols stand for speech. Like other soft neurological signs, comprehension problems serve as an indication that the brain of a dyslexic child is not functioning like that of a normal reader.

Inability to write coherently. Children who have difficulty understanding the stories in their books usually also have difficulty putting their thoughts into writing. Coherent stories have a recognizable structure—usually a beginning, middle, and end—but the stories written by some dyslexic children are a jumble of thoughts and impressions. There is little, if any, story line, characters are confused, and events are disorganized.

Many of these children cannot deliver aloud a coherent story and have problems describing everyday events— what they did over the weekend, a school field trip, etc. It's not that these children are unaware of or indifferent to their experiences; researchers believe that children give sketchy, incomplete, and confusing explanations when they are unable to use spoken or written language to express themselves. Like impaired reading comprehension, the inability to write coherent stories suggests to many experts that the brain of a dyslexic child functions in fundamentally different ways from that of a child who does not have reading problems.

DYSLEXIA—
A DIAGNOSIS WITHOUT A PRESCRIPTION

The problems reading-disabled children have dealing with print are so debilitating that they cannot make progress unless they receive a great deal of carefully designed and expertly delivered reading instruction. Dyslexic children are eligible for special educational programs offered by schools. That these children need extra help goes without saying. The problem comes with the label.

Once diagnosed "dyslexic," the label doesn't have much value as a teaching tool. That is, teachers who have a dyslexic child in their classrooms cannot select with certainty the most effective educational approach. Upon determining that two children have pneumonia, physicians can prescribe antibiotics with the expectations that the disease will be cured. Upon being told that two children are labeled dyslexic, teachers cannot expect a single teaching method to be equally successful with each child. Because dyslexia remains a mystery, teachers must be able to use a number of different educational techniques and must be willing to try a number of different approaches with the same child.

THREE CONDITIONS
WHICH COMPLICATE DYSLEXIA

In addition to exhibiting severe reading problems, dyslexic children often have accompanying problems that further complicate learning. The difference between children who learn normally and those who do not is in the severity and duration of these complicating behaviors. If your child is failing to learn to read and shows one of these three complications, request an evaluation by the school's psychologist. And maybe there is no cause for worry. Every now and then I see my own children do one of these three things, but never severely enough or for long enough to affect achievement in school.

Is your child noticeably more active than other children the same age? Hyperactivity is a term used to describe overly energetic children. Hyperactivity goes beyond causing poor work habits. Driven by a compelling need for movement, hyperactive children are in constant, and frequently inappropriate, ill-timed motion. As you can imagine, the impact of hyperactivity on learning is alarming.

I once worked with a second-grader whose teacher had been giving him extra help, yet he had made little progress. Frustrated by putting in intensive teaching effort with little to show for it, Richard's teacher asked me to visit her classroom in order to see if I could give her some helpful suggestions. I sat in the corner of the classroom for thirty minutes watching Richard as he worked. Among other things, Richard spent a lot of his time rummaging through his desk, pestering the children on either side of him, tipping his seat over (he did this twice), dropping his pencils, and kicking his feet. Several times, he got up from his desk to wander around the room. Once he got into a tussle with another child over who would get to the pencil sharpener first. Richard wasn't able to settle down for even five minutes of sustained work. Not one paper—not even a short spelling assignment—was completed in thirty minutes of class time.

Because excessively active children are constantly in motion, they cannot settle down long enough to learn to read or do much else where controlling body movement is required. Activity is a healthy part of childhood, and normal children have plenty of energy. But unlike normal activity which fits comfortably into a child's everyday routine, hyperactivity is disturbing. Hyperactive children display inappropriate behavior in both social and classroom settings—they cannot sit still in movie theaters, are unable to remain still or quiet in cars, and are compelled to move about excessively in their classrooms.

Hyperactivity has such a disruptive effect on classroom life that teachers are quick to inform parents of signs of it in their children. Few children are hyperactive, but those who are need special education plans. As children move through the elementary grades, hyperactivity often subsides. However, if the level of activity cannot be satisfactorily managed during the early years, a severe reading deficit is likely to remain long after hyperactivity has disappeared.

Medication is available, but not all children respond positively to it, and *opinion is divided as to its long-term benefits.* Ritalin (methylphenidate) is the drug most often prescribed by physicians; Dexedrine (dextroamphetamine) is another commonly used drug. (Dexedrine, the diet pill pepper-upper for adults, often has an opposite, calming effect on children.) Those who believe that medication is beneficial suggest that excessive behavior is reduced and attention to classroom tasks is increased. Those opposed point to negative side effects, including loss of appetite or disturbed sleep patterns, when dosages are incorrect. For those children who respond favorably to medication, the effects of hyperactivity usually return when medication is discontinued.

Some physicians and parents have become convinced that certain food substances are linked to hyperactivity. The use of diet to control hyperactivity was popularized in 1975 by a book entitled *Why Your Child is Hyperactive* (71). The author recommended that reducing certain food substances and omitting others would reduce activity levels and improve attention to classroom tasks. For some children, products like sugar, caffeine, and certain preservatives may act as stimulants. After eating foods high in these compounds, children may become excitable, irritable, or overly active.

However, not all physicians agree with restricting children's diets, and much of the evidence in support of the connection between food compounds, dyslexia, and hyperactivity does not meet the rigorous research standards set by the medical profession. Food allergies are commonplace and don't usually interfere with learning. I have a friend who gets horrible headaches when she eats chocolate cake made from certain brands of mixes, yet the ingredients in cake mixes haven't had a negative effect on her learning. On the other hand, children who become overly active when certain food substances are eaten might benefit from diets that restrict troublesome compounds.

This doesn't mean that food substances *cause* hyperactivity or dyslexia, only that certain foods may worsen its effects. If eating a candy bar results in increased activity and less attention paid to classroom tasks, candy bars should be avoided. What we must keep in mind is that eliminating food compounds from our children's diets won't change the way their minds process written words. However, changing their diets may help them to take advantage of the learning potential they have. Herein lies the primary advantage of sensitivity to diet. To the extent that the things children eat cause them to be fidgety, sullen, or aggressive, learning in school can be enhanced when certain foods are avoided.

Can your child concentrate on classroom work? By their nature, hyperactive children do not concentrate on classroom assignments. Still, there is another kind of child who is not overly active yet is unable to get much done. This kind of child sits at his desk, his mind a thousand miles away. He has great difficulty paying attention. His power of concentration is so limited that his thoughts can focus on a single task for only a few minutes at a time.

When I think about children who have problems concentrating, I am reminded of a little girl I worked with several years ago. Bette was a pleasant, rather quiet child. She sat in her seat all day long and accomplished almost nothing. She would begin an assignment, erase her name and begin again, make a letter too large, get a new sheet of paper and try a second time. She spent a lot of time looking up words in her dictionary and was sidetracked by other activities. Sometimes she would daydream, sitting and staring into space. It wasn't that Bette was bored, which might have explained her inattentiveness; she behaved the same way in Girl Scouts, in Sunday school, and on the soccer field.

Children like Bette cannot concentrate in or out of school. Not only are they unable to focus on school work, they cannot attend to leisure activities like building model airplanes, putting together puzzles, or playing cards. Children who cannot pay attention for even short periods of time need specialized help.

If your child's teacher thinks that your child is behind in his school work because of an inability to pay attention, and if inattention is a problem noticed consistently by adults who interact with your child in nonschool settings, consult your school psychologist and look into the matter.

Does your child talk as well as other children in your neighborhood? Difficulty with spoken language and severe reading problems occur together with such frequency that delayed language development in preschoolers is interpreted as a sign that children may be at risk of reading failure. This is due to the strong tie that experts find between reading comprehension problems, memory impairments, and difficulties processing spoken language. Children who have a language disability, or who are delayed in their development of language, have underdeveloped speaking vocabularies, and experience great difficulties understanding spoken requests, expressing themselves in conversations, and using language to communicate their desires and opinions.

There are several things you can look for, the most important being a strange or illogical ordering of ideas. In this instance, your child's speech becomes difficult to understand because the ideas are garbled and confused. Another related problem that you should watch for is a tendency to make an unusually large number of grammatical errors. Even when parents and teachers place a high value on good grammar, certain children are unable to remember correct language usage. In the normal course of development, children use and discard many incorrect grammatical expressions. You should be aware of persistent problems with grammar that continue even when other children no longer seem to be having difficulty. While you are listening for a logical arrangement of ideas and grammatically correct usage, listen, too, for speaking fluency. Some children experience a mental block when they are unable to find the right word. Their speech is characterized by hesitations as these children search for the words they want to use.

If you see your child exhibiting any one of these three complicating behaviors with any routine frequency, and if your child is having reading problems, call the child's teacher about beginning an aggressive remedial plan. Make sure to involve the school psychologist, since a team of experts is often necessary.

With or without these three complications, it takes time to overcome a serious learning disability. Children and parents must be patient, and educational efforts have to be continuous. The important role we play as parents in our children's education, and the positive impact of early intervention, cannot be overemphasized.

9

DOS AND DON'TS FOR HELPING YOUR CHILD AT HOME

Not all teachers are parents, but all parents are teachers.
—*William J. Bennett, former U.S. Secretary
of Education, in* First Lessons *(72)*

Here are a few tried and true Dos for working at home with your child, along with some mistakes that should be avoided—the Don'ts.

DOS: GOOD THINGS
TO DO WITH CHILDREN AT HOME

- *Do* encourage your child to use all sorts of colored pencils and pens. Magic Markers, crayons, colored ballpoint pens—any medium your child enjoys. Colored pencils and pens are a special treat since they are not usually permitted in school.
- Work with your child in short segments of time. For children in the first and second grade, ten to fifteen

minutes is enough. Older children can sustain attention longer, perhaps up to twenty or thirty minutes.

- *Do* tell children whenever they're correct—letting
  them know when they're right is one of the cardinal
  principles of good instruction, a principle teachers
  have been using successfully for years.
- When your child makes a mistake, wait a moment to
  allow him to correct himself. If the mistake is not corrected, give your child the right answer and go on with
  the lesson. Providing the right answer when your child
  falters makes your home helping relationship relaxed
  and free of tension.
- *Do* vary your routine. Change the order of activities
  you use frequently; change the location where you
  work with your child; change learning activities.
- Use chalkboards and colored chalk. Small chalkboards
  are a terrific substitute for paper. Colored chalk has
  lots of appeal and is easily erased. Both are inexpensive
  and add extra spice to learning activities.
- Let your child choose some of the learning activities.
  For example, if you are trying to build your child's
  reading vocabulary, give a choice of two or three word-
  learning activities. Selecting some of the activities allows children to take charge of their own learning and
  helps ensure their commitment to the activities chosen.
- *Do* solicit help from other family members—brothers,
  sisters, grandmothers, and grandfathers. Anyone your
  child has good rapport with is a potential helper. Include other family members in learning activities when
  possible and encourage your child to share learning
  with interested adults in the family. Once your child
  understands how learning activities work, it's a great
  confidence booster to show grandmother and grand-
  father the wonderful things he is learning.
- *Do* give your child a few minutes to calm down and

become oriented to learning activities before you begin. Shifting from play to reading activities may require some time. Begin with an easy activity that gives your child the time he needs to settle down and ensure that learning gets off to a good start.

- Tell your child's classroom teacher about what you are doing at home. It's important to keep the teacher informed so that she can take your home activities into account when planning classroom lessons.

- *Do* ask your child's teacher for suggestions. You will get all sorts of good ideas: word lists, suggestions for books to read at home, specific reading abilities your child needs to master, the kinds of activities your child especially enjoys.

- Always include one easy activity when you help your child. Easy activities are great confidence builders and terrific motivators.

- Feel free to change home learning activities any way you would like. None of the ideas in this book are inviolable. If, for whatever reason, you or your child feel uncomfortable with a learning activity, modify it. If modification doesn't work, discard it and try another.

- Always remember that you know your child far better than a classroom teacher, school psychologist, or pediatrician. Rely on your own judgment about the things your child will and will not do, does and does not enjoy.

- If your child has trouble paying attention, shorten the time you spend on learning activities and offer rewards for your child's efforts. For example, if your child is looking for words in a vocabulary learning activity, give him a small token like a bottle cap for every three words found. At the end of the work time, bottle caps can be traded for extra privileges. Fifteen bottle caps might be exchanged for an extra dessert, thirty for an extra television show on the weekend.

- *Do* set aside a special place for your child to keep papers, pencils, school books. A cardboard box will do, or an inexpensive plastic milk crate. I prefer milk crates because they are stackable (a space-saving device), and their colorful latticed sides mean that the contents of each crate can be seen without unloading every time you want to find something.

- *Do* keep a family dictionary, atlas, and almanac handy, and help your child to use these references to locate answers to homework questions.

- Encourage your child to be responsible for making decisions about his daily schedule. Children who are responsible for planning how and when they will accomplish daily tasks learn to make wise decisions about the use of time. Developing a sense of responsibility is crucial for learning, at home and at school.

- *Do* encourage the expression of feelings. Learning that is challenging and mind-engaging is accompanied by many different emotions—excitement, encouragement, frustration, satisfaction. Acknowledge these feelings and accept them as the healthy signs of a solid home learning connection. By establishing an open, sharing relationship, you and your child can share the joy and work out the difficulties that may arise from working closely with one another.

DON'TS: THINGS TO
AVOID WITH CHILDREN AT HOME

- *Don't* be intimidated by what other parents tell you about their own children. Neither you nor your child need to measure yourselves by someone else's yardstick for success. Perhaps the most debilitating thing about discussing our children with other parents is listening to them boast and describe in detail their children's accomplishments. Mario may have read one hundred books, Frederick sixty, your child ten. Don't let these kinds of facts discourage you. Learning to read need not be competitive, although some parents would have you think otherwise. Praise your child for his accomplishments, congratulate yourself and the teacher for your child's successes, and set aside the self-serving comments of other parents. Your child is working toward a goal that is uniquely his own— reaching a personal potential to be a skilled reader.

- Avoid substituting home learning activities for recreational activities your child values. Helping your child at home is best accomplished when learning activities are introduced in addition to normal leisure-time activities, not in lieu of recreational activities.

- When you work with your child, be sensitive to what other children in the family are doing. If everyone else is sitting on the back porch eating popcorn while your child is working with you, the home learning connection isn't going to work. On the other hand, if the other children are doing homework while you are helping your child with reading, your child will not feel excluded from a special treat.

- Avoid comparing your child to other siblings, neighborhood children, or relatives. Treat your child as a unique, special person. Applaud his accomplishments and help him to shore up his weaknesses.

- *Don't* force your child to finish an activity if interest is lost. More harm than good comes from forced completion of a learning activity children find boring or frustrating.

- Consider the room in which you work. Reading in a room full of distractions is a big mistake. Your home learning connection will not be successful if you try to work with your child in a room where others are talking, watching television, listening to the radio, or playing with toys. Noise should be kept to a minimum. Turn off the television and radio, or move to a room without them.

- *Don't* greet your child at the door after school with comments like "How was reading today? Did you get all your papers right? Did you miss any words?" It is a very fine line that separates healthy concern from pressure to perform in your child's mind. If you are quick to question or focus too much attention on how things are going at school, your child will perceive that you are uneasy about progress in school. The next thing you know, your child is putting up his guard when you ask school-related questions. This kind of behavior leads to answers like "Nothing" or "I don't know." That you be concerned with your child's progress in school is desirable; that you express too much concern is counterproductive. When your child comes home, wait awhile before asking about the day. Varying the questions you ask about school will also be helpful.

- If you don't like a particular learning activity, do not use it with your child. Your negative feelings about an exercise will come through without saying a word. Successful activities are those that both you and your child enjoy. There are plenty of learning activities from which to choose in this book; discard those you find unappealing.

- Be careful about overloading your child with obligations. Scouts, soccer, Little League, and art class are all mind-expanding extracurricular activities, but some choices should be made. Too many extra activities will leave your child with no time and little energy for family life. Work at striking a balance between extra activities, time with family, and time spent on homework and on home learning activities. One mother I know limits her elementary school daughters to two out-of-school activities per week; my own children are permitted to participate in one extra activity during the school year and two during the summer.

- Above all, don't feel you've failed if your child doesn't want to work with you on a particular day. No child will want to work with Mom or Dad every single day, nor is there any child in a classroom who is enthusiastic about school lessons all the time. I do not mean to imply that if your child tells you he doesn't want to learn more about reading you simply drop the idea. On the other hand, from time to time all children tire of learning activities at home and at school. When this happens, wait a few days or even a few weeks before resuming reading activities.

10

PHONICS LEARNING ACTIVITIES

Everything we know about how children learn to read tells us that phonics is crucial for getting off to a good start. Phonics gives your child a means of changing written words he has never seen into spoken words he recognizes from conversation. Once pronounced, written words are easily understood and remembered. This makes an understanding of phonics a shortcut for word learning and an indispensable tool for children in the elementary grades.

By the time they are nine years old, American children know enough words to read independently. Not only have they built a strong reading vocabulary, but owing to a good knowledge of phonics most youngsters can sound out for themselves many of the new words in their books. Although phonics is crucial for unlocking the pronunciation of written words, not all languages have a similar key.

Children learning Chinese, a language that uses characters to represent spoken words, must be able to remember a whole spoken word for each unique Chinese character. For the purpose of everyday reading, Chinese youngsters need to know between 4,000 and 7,000 characters. Remembering such a large number of different character—spoken word connections requires a great deal of effort and many years of schooling.

What makes learning English words faster and easier for beginning readers is the fact that each letter of the alphabet stands for a sound. Children who are skilled at using phonics can take full advantage of the shortcut our alphabet provides. Those who do not understand phonics must learn individual words just as Chinese youngsters learn characters, and the benefit of the alphabet is lost.

HOW SOON, HOW MUCH?

How soon should your child learn phonics? To my way of thinking, the sooner the better. Given a good knowledge of phonics, your child will have a larger reading vocabulary, better comprehension, and stand on higher tiers of the reading pyramid than the child who doesn't learn phonics early on.

Knowledge of phonics is so important that it is questionable whether your child can become a successful reader without it. Children who have an underdeveloped ability to use phonics can take many, many years to learn to read. Those who cannot use phonics at all seldom read beyond the beginning first-grade level.

Teaching phonics to beginning readers is the very best way to ensure good reading achievement. At no other time in the elementary grades is phonics as critical as it is when children are standing on the first three tiers of the reading pyramid. This makes it imperative to teach phonics in the early elementary grades, the time when children depend on phonics the most.

Beginning readers rely heavily on phonics because they encounter a great many new words in their storybooks. I was reminded of this fact one afternoon as I watched a first-grade teacher read a library book to her class. While most of the children listened with fascination to their teacher, several boys began to talk. After a while, the discussion grew so loud that the teacher put the book in her lap. Looking up she said to the class, "Do you have any idea why I'm not reading?" "Sure," answered one of the girls in a most insightful tone. "There's a word you don't know and you're going to sound it out."

From a beginning reader's point of view, this was a perfectly logical answer. Seeing a new word in her storybook, this little girl does what all beginning readers do—she uses phonics to sound out the word. While study after study supports the notion that phonics should be taught early and taught well, phonics instruction does have its limits.

As children climb higher up the reading pyramid, less phonics instruction is necessary; children in the upper elementary grades do not depend on phonics as beginning readers do. For the most part, fourth-, fifth-, and sixth-graders can already read a great many words in their library books and subject-matter textbooks. As a consequence, older, more able readers don't have reason to use phonics as frequently as younger, less skilled readers. Older children are also more skilled at using the information contained in a sentence as a clue to unknown words. Combining information from a sentence with a knowledge of phonics results in a powerful word-recognition tool that allows readers to bypass the time-consuming process of sounding out each single letter-sound combination in a word.

The better the reader, the smaller the contribution phonics makes. Highly skilled adult readers seldom use phonics. Most of the words we read on a day-to-day basis are words we already know. Of course, phonics is always available as a backup, but sounding out words is probably not a major part of our normal everyday reading.

That phonics must be taught in the early elementary

grades, then, is very clear. What is less clear, though, is how much phonics instruction children need to become good readers. Like a swinging pendulum, teachers have favored heavy phonics instruction, then less, and back again to a lot.

Early in this century, phonics had a prominent place in the elementary school program and was a fundamental part of classroom reading lessons. A lot of time went into teaching phonics, and children were expected to know a great deal about the relationship between letters and sounds. But over the years the emphasis on phonics declined. Although instruction in phonics was never completely dropped from elementary reading programs, during the 1950s comparatively little phonics instruction found its way into classrooms.

By the early 1960s, the pendulum began to swing in the opposite direction, and the emphasis on phonics began to rise. The popularity of phonics as a teaching tool continued to increase to the point it has reached today as an integral part of every reading program. If children aren't getting enough phonics in their day-to-day reading lessons, teachers have a wealth of supplementary workbooks and materials to which they can turn.

Although your child will learn more phonics than the children of three decades ago, there still isn't agreement on exactly how much phonics instruction is optimum. The pendulum may be swinging away from an emphasis on phonics instruction, for many reading authorities are critical of the amount of time spent on it. The chances are high that less phonics will be taught in the future.

PHONICS ESSENTIALS

If every letter of our alphabet stood for only one sound, phonics would be easy. But there are more sounds in English than we have letters in our alphabet. With only twenty-six letters and over forty sounds, certain letters are bound to end up representing several sounds. This is the reason there are so many rules and examples to teach your child about the nature of letter-sound relationships.

I have described what I believe are the seven most necessary, essential things to learn about phonics. Phonics essentials are important because your child is guaranteed to use them every day and to learn them in school. Admittedly, there is a lot more to phonics than the seven essentials described in this chapter, yet by learning these essentials, your child will have the knowledge necessary to sound out a great many of the words in his storybooks.

Since it is receiving greater emphasis in today's classrooms, your child will undoubtedly learn more about phonics than is covered by these seven essentials. If you want to go beyond the essentials, ask your child's teacher for suggestions. She can tell you about the phonics skills your child is working on in class and those that might be practiced at home.

When you talk to your child's teacher, you are likely to hear her use special phonics terms. In order to understand the teacher when she describes your child's progress and how phonics essentials work, you'll need to know the meaning of these terms. You'll find six new terms described in the phonics essentials that follow. Two of them, **consonants** and **vowels,** are explained in the first essential.

Essential 1. Consonant sounds. The twenty-six letters of our alphabet are divided into two groups—one of twenty-one consonants, and one of five vowels. The vowels are **a, e, i, o,** and **u** (sometimes **y** is also a vowel); the rest of the letters are consonants.

Because consonants are easier to learn than vowels, my suggestion is to teach consonant letters first. Consonants provide the basic structure for words; even without the vowels, we can figure out the words in this sentence: Th_

Lttl_ g_rl r_d_ h_r b_k_. Consonant letters alone give you the clues you need. When the same sentence is rewritten to include only vowel letters, it's more difficult, if not impossible, to figure out the words: __e _i__e _i__ _o_e _e_ _i_e.

Perhaps more imprtant, consonant letters stand for fewer sounds than vowel letters. If your child knows the sound of the consonant letter **t,** he will have no difficulty with it in words like **tape, rattle,** and **cart.** Your child will find it relatively easy to learn this predictable letter-sound combination. Unlike **t,** the vowel letter **a** represents a different sound in each of those three words. Knowing the sound of **a** in **tape** won't help your child figure out the pronunciation of **rattle** and **cart.**

Consonants are straightforward and easy to learn, and I seldom meet a child who doesn't know them. Even remedial readers know consonant sounds, particularly when they come at the beginning of a word. Maida, a fifth-grader, typifies the frequency with which remedial readers learn consonants before vowels.

When she was ten years old, Maida was still reading on a first-grade level. She knew very few written words and struggled through everything she attempted to read. But Maida knew consonant sounds. When she came to a word she didn't know, she had the phonics knowledge to figure out the beginning consonant sound—but that was as far as she could go. Maida knew little else about phonics.

Perhaps the reason Maida, and other children like her, learned consonant sounds so readily is due in part to the fact that consonants usually come at the beginning of words. Their placement at the beginning of words causes children's attention to be focused immediately on consonant letters, often in hopes of getting a helpful clue about the word's pronunciation.

One hundred of the 129 words in the two paragraphs you just read begin with consonants. Knowing the sound of a beginning consonant gets your child on the right track for sounding out a word.

Suppose the first time your child sees the word **tub** is in this sentence: **James fell headfirst into the tub.** If your child knows the sound of the beginning consonant **t,** he will automatically understand that this new word couldn't possibly be **rub** or **scrub.** After deciding how the word **tub** begins, your child's next step is to figure out the rest of the sounds in the word. This is where vowels letters become important.

Essential 2. Short and long vowel letter sounds. The first thing your child needs to learn about vowels is that each one has both a short sound and a long sound. Short sounds are the **a** in **apple,** the **e** in **elephant,** the **i** in **igloo,** the **o** in **ostrich,** and the **u** in **umbrella.** The **a** in **safe** is a long sound, as is the **e** in **beet,** the **o** in **boat,** and the **u** in **tube.**

If the idea that vowel letters have more than one sound sounds potentially confusing to you, think how confusing it is for your child! One day recently, I stopped by the desk of a little girl who was writing a letter to her grandparents. What caught my eye was the way Emily had spelled grandpa. "Grandpa," she told me, "is spelled **g-r-a-n-d-p-o.**" "Grandpa," I replied, "ends in an **a,** not an **o.**" "Vowels," she sighed in disgust, "are always messing me up!" Emily's right—vowels can mess children up for a long time. It takes at least through the second grade, sometimes longer, for children to get vowel sounds straight.

The most efficient way to teach short and long vowel sounds is to focus on the way that words are spelled. Teach your child when he sees words with a single vowel between consonants, like **can, did, got, had, spell,** and **lot,** that he should expect a short vowel sound. Many of the words your child reads, especially as a beginning reader, are going to be short words spelled like this.

For long vowel sounds, there are three signals worth

teaching your child. The first signal is seeing two vowels side by side, like the **oa** in **boat** or the **ee** in **feet.** When one vowel is immediately followed by another, the first is usually long, the second silent. Some teachers explain it like this: "When two vowels go walking the first one does the talking (has a long sound) and the second one does the walking (is silent)." In order to be a good reader your child will need to know the sound of the **ai** (in **mail**), **ay** (in **play**), **ea** (in **treat**), **ee** (in **beet**), and **oa** (in **coat**).

Seeing a word spelled with a vowel followed by a consonant and a final **e,** as in **take, ride, like,** and **flute,** is a second long vowel signal. Your child should know that in most words spelled with a vowel, consonant, and final **e,** the first vowel is long and the final **e** is silent. The final **e** is the key to this signal. By adding a final **e,** words with short vowel sounds, like **mat, pet, hid, rod,** and **tub,** become words with long vowel sounds—**mate, Pete, hide, rode,** and **tube.**

The last long vowel signal to teach your child pertains to short words such as **we, she, go,** and **hi.** When short words are spelled with only one vowel, and that vowel comes at the end, your child should expect a long vowel sound. This is an instance in which **y** is a vowel. Teach your child that words like **try, fly,** and **by** have long vowel sounds.

Essential 3. R-controlled vowels. After helping a great many children with phonics, I have come to appreciate the importance of teaching about the letter **r.** When an **r** comes after a vowel, the **r** often dominates the vowel sound we hear—hence the name "r-controlled vowel." The **ar** in **part, er** in **sister, ir** in **skirt, or** in **story,** and **ur** in **turn** are examples of r-controlled vowel sounds. If you can't hear any difference between the **er, ir,** and **ur,** you're right—the r-controlled vowels sound alike in these words!

R-controlled vowels are the product of shifts in English

pronunciation that occurred several hundred years ago. In order to make vowels easier to pronounce, the sounds of the vowel and **r** were folded together, the result being that r-controlled vowels have neither a long nor a short sound. Your child will learn to read hundreds of words that include r-controlled vowels. Known words provide excellent examples of this essential, like **car, farm, her, paper, third, first, for, horse, turn,** and **hurt.** As one might imagine, spelling presents a greater problem. The r-controlled vowels **er, ir,** and **ur** offer no sound clues to spellers, so that the correct spelling of words containing these letter combinations must be memorized.

Essential 4. Vowel diphthongs. Diphthongs (pronounced *dif*-thong) are two consecutive vowels both of which contribute to the sounds heard in words. Although diphthongs are vowel combinations, their sounds differ from long and short vowels, and they do not follow the pattern for side-by-side vowels—the first vowel is long, the second silent (as in **oa** in **boat**). There are four diphthongs: **oi, oy, ou,** and **ow. Oi** and **oy** represent the sounds heard in the words **boil** and **boy, ou** and **ow** the sounds in **found** and **how.** Examples of words with diphthongs include **join, choice, joy, oyster, out, proud, cow,** and **town.** Your child will learn diphthongs more quickly if you teach **oi-oy** and **ou-ow** as pairs. Since each pair stands for the same sound, it is easier to learn them together.

Because vowels have a great many sounds, it won't be surprising to learn that **ow** also stands for a long **o** sound in words like **snow** and **throw. Ow** is classified as a diphthong only when it has the sounds of **ow** in **brown** and **clown.** My advice is to teach your child first to try the sound in **town.** If that sound doesn't work, try the long **o** sound.

Essential 5. Consonant blends. When two or more letters are pronounced closely together, the outcome is called a blend. It is important for your child to learn blends because they, too, often come at the beginning of many words. Most blends in English include the letters **r, l,** or **s.** Blends with the letter **r** include **br, cr, dr, fr, gr, pr,** and **tr.** The letter **l** is used in **bl, cl, fl, pl, sl,** and **spl. S** is part of **sc, scr, sk, sm, sn, sp, spr, st, str, squ,** and **sw.**

Essential 6. Diagraphs. Like blends, diagraphs are made up of more than one letter. But unlike blends, diagraphs stand for only one sound, and the sound of diagraphs may be completely new. Diagraphs with vowels might be the **au** in **taught,** the **aw** in **saw,** or the **oo** in **school** or **took.** Diagraphs with consonants include the **ch** in **cheer** and **Christmas, ph** in **phone, sh** in **she, th** in **there** and **thank, wh** in **who, ng** in **sing, nk** in **drink,** and **ck** in **sick.** Blends will be easier for your child to learn than diagraphs. For this reason, I suggest you begin by teaching blends and shift then to diagraphs.

Essential 7. Word endings. In first and second grades, your child will learn special word endings, or suffixes. Word endings your child will need to know are **s, ed, ing, ly, er, est, ful, less** and **ous.** Adding **s, ed,** and **ing** to **walk,** we get **walks, walked,** and **walking. Ly, er,** and **est** change **nice** to **nicely, nicer,** and **nicest. Joy** becomes **joyful, joyless,** and **joyous** when **ful, less,** and **ous** are added. Teach **s, ed,** and **ing** first, then teach the rest.

Children who are just beginning to read or who are having difficulty learning to read sometimes may think that a word with one of these endings is completely new. I've watched many children puzzle over words ending with an **ed** or **ing.** Because an ending makes a word look different, less-skilled readers have the impression they don't know that word. The point you want to make to your child is that words with endings aren't new—they're the same words your child already knows, but with something special added.

WHAT IS THE BEST ORDER
FOR LEARNING PHONICS ESSENTIALS?

Should your child learn short vowels before long vowels, or r-controlled vowels before diphthongs? I can't offer you the easiest learning sequence because there isn't any solid evidence favoring one way of ordering phonics essentials over another. While we know that consonants are easier to learn than vowels and that blends are less troublesome than diagraphs, this is precious little knowledge to come out of over a hundred years of experience teaching phonics.

In the absence of a firm set of guidelines, publishers of reading programs devise their own order for teaching phonics essentials. In classrooms in which reading is taught with the whole-language approach, teachers may choose to change the sequence from one child to another so that what is learned about phonics meets the needs of each child individually. Sometimes school districts, like the one in Prince Georges County, Maryland, develop excellent phonics programs of their own. Because every school's program teaches phonics essentials in a different order, my advice is to follow the sequence of the program your child's school uses. Ask your child's teacher for the phonics skills included in the school's reading program. That way you are assured of being in step with the kinds of phonics essentials your child is learning in the classroom.

INVENTED SPELLING

There is a powerful relationship between reading and writing. Lots of practice writing makes for better reading ability, and better reading results in improved writing skills.

As one of the language arts, writing is a skill we all want our children to learn.

Much criticism has been leveled at American schools because they graduate high school students who write poorly. This criticism is certainly justified. In years past, many of the students in my university classes have been woefully lacking in the ability to write. If we want our children to write better, we must do the things that result in better writing. One thing we do know about learning to write is that children who write early and write often become the best writers.

Knowing this, my daughter's teacher, like all the teachers in her northern Virginia school, encourages the children in her first-grade classroom to write every day. Most of the words the children in my daughter's class want to write are words that they do not know how to spell. If the children in the class had to use letter-perfect spelling, they wouldn't write anything, but my daughter's teacher sets aside her red pencil and encourages the children to use their knowledge of phonics to spell.

At first, many beginning readers spell words just the way they sound. The term used to describe this phenomenon is "invented spelling." Children seem to pass through several stages on their way to becoming skilled spellers. Most begin by stringing together a collection of random letters, such as **smprn** for the word **letter.** At the next stage, children write letters that represent the beginning and/or ending sounds of words, as in **lr** for **letter.** You are likely to see this kind of spelling on the papers that many kindergartners bring home from school. As kindergarten and first-grade children learn more about vowel and consonant letter-sound associations, they begin to spell words just as the words sound. Children who have progressed to this third stage might spell the word **letter** as **letr.** In the fourth stage, a transition between spelling words as they sound and letter-perfect spelling, children combine phonics knowledge with visual memory for letter patterns in words. Children at this stage would perhaps spell **letter** as **leter.** Correct spelling, the fifth and last stage, emerges when children's knowledge of letter-sound relationships and visual memory are perfected. If your child is a kindergartner or first- or second-grader, you are likely to read creative stories in which spelling reflects one or more of these stages. Movement is gradual from one stage to the next, and the process of becoming an expert speller involves much practice.

Invented spelling is an accepted practice in kindergarten and first-grade classrooms today—it is fundamental to the whole-language approach and is a natural outgrowth of learning phonics. The idea is to use invented spelling as a temporary bridge between the words a child wants to write and the words a child knows how to spell. If your child is in kindergarten or first grade, you probably see examples of invented spelling all the time. If your child writes the word **camra** on his list of possible birthday presents, as mine did, this kind of spelling is perfectly natural.

I never tire of reading children's renditions of how the alphabet should work. When Rosa wrote to her grandmother, she asked for some **stuft** toys for her birthday. Since Rosa had not yet learned the **ed** word ending, she wrote "stuffed" as she heard it—with the sound of the letter **t.** Rosa also wanted a **woch** (watch). According to the seven phonics essentials, the way Rosa spells watch makes perfectly good sense!

Perhaps you find yourself flinching a bit when I talk about "making up" spelling. English spelling is challenging enough; why let children make it more complex by inventing new ways to spell? If children were permitted to invent spelling throughout the elementary grades, I would be among the first to advocate that a stop be put to such a practice. But by second grade most children have learned to spell enough words so that they can write without using invented spelling, and invented spelling is then supplanted by traditional spelling.

WHEN PHONICS DOESN'T WORK

It will probably come as no surprise to hear that not all words can be sounded out using phonics. Because we have borrowed words from other languages, and because English spelling has not always kept current with shifts in pronunciation, some words are not spelled as they sound— **said, once,** and **were,** for example—and therefore phonics isn't a completely dependable means of learning new words.

When you use the learning activities in this chapter, it is important to select only those words that will work with phonics. If you are uncertain as to whether or not a word will work, see if you can pronounce it using the seven phonics essentials. If you can, it's a workable word. Fortunately, the majority of words don't stray far from the seven phonics essentials, and most of the time, phonics will provide your child with a good shortcut for learning words. I have supplied examples of words that follow the seven phonics essentials—a list for younger readers and one for older readers. The library books that your child reads for pleasure and the textbooks that he uses to complete his homework assignments are both excellent sources of words that can be used in phonics learning activities. A quick inspection of these books is likely to yield plenty of useful words. Many of the textbooks for older readers include glossaries—excellent sources of words—while others list important words at the ends of chapters.

WORDS THAT FOLLOW THE PHONICS ESSENTIALS

Words for Younger Readers		*Words for Older Readers*	
after	made/make	absurd	lean
ate	man/men	amaze	least

best	me/my	amount	loaf
big	name	appeal	marsh
brown	not	avoid	moan
came	out	breach	perhaps
cat	place	brisk	person
can	ran/run	border	provide
clean	red	burst	publish
did	ride	comment	realize
down	same	complain	reflect
each	see	consider	remain
first	she	decide	rude
fly	side	despite	scarf
gave	sleep	dismay	scarlet
got	stop	dragon	scowl
green	take	drew	silent
had	time	entire	spice
home	town	escape	splendid
how	try	fault	swift
jump	up	freedom	tilt
just	wait	gaze	tramp
keep	water	growl	tribe
like	white	grim	vain
look	wish	invade	vanish

Even when words can be sounded out using phonics, your child must know the word in speech before phonics serves a real purpose. Sounding out the word **pepper** works for two reasons: first, **pepper** is spelled just like it sounds, and second, **pepper** is a common enough word that your child is bound to recognize it when he says it. **Peptic,** on the other hand, poses a different problem.

If your child doesn't already know the word **peptic** in speech, sounding it out won't trigger a response. Phonics cannot tell your child what a word means, only how it sounds. Once he pronounces it, your child will still have to go to the dictionary to find out what **peptic** means. From a practical standpoint, it's important to use the learning activities in this chapter in conjunction with words your child is guaranteed to recognize once they are sounded out.

WILL YOUR CHILD BENEFIT FROM EXTRA HELP?

Perhaps you aren't sure whether or not your child might benefit from extra help at home. You won't be surprised to hear that less-able readers—children who are reading far below the level of their classmates—are likely to profit from extra help with phonics, vocabulary, and comprehension. Average readers in the lower elementary grades may benefit from these activities as well. Children who are making average progress in the upper elementary grades are likely to benefit from additional help with vocabulary and comprehension, since these two areas present the greater challenges to children in grades four through six. Extra help may not be necessary for exceptionally good readers (children who read well beyond the level of their classmates).

All children, from the most able reader to the least, will profit from reading in a variety of genres (biography, poetry, mystery, etc.) and from the book-sharing activities described in Chapter 3. Extra help with phonics, vocabulary, and comprehension will be more effective, too, when used in conjunction with wide reading and book sharing.

These learning activities can be readily adapted to your child's level of reading ability—more difficult for average and good readers, easier for less-able readers. When a learning activity is likely to appeal only to younger or older children, it will be noted in the description of the activity. The activities are intended to provide effective instruction that is both challenging and enjoyable, without the paper and pencil seat work that may be used some of the time in elementary classrooms. I'd suggest consulting your child's teacher for specific guidance about the areas that would be most beneficial, and then allowing your child to select the activities from an area that he enjoys.

LEARNING ACTIVITIES

The nine phonics learning activities that follow look more like games than the traditional drill and practice worksheets you might normally associate with phonics. The aim of the exercises is to provide your child with valuable practice while at the same time ensuring that the learning experience is positive and successful. Activities that are like games accomplish this best. As with the other learning activities in this book, use only those your child enjoys and only as long as learning is fun.

1. TIC-TAC-TOE
Combining tic-tac-toe with phonics makes for a great learning game that may appeal to children of any age. Suppose you're helping your child to learn blends. You and your child each select a blend—perhaps your child likes the **bl** blend and you pick **st.** Rather than putting X's and O's in the squares, your child writes words with **st** blends and you write words with **bl** blends. The drawing shows a sample game in which the player who chose the **bl** blend won the game. If your child needs help thinking of words with **st,** write a few examples on a piece of paper. Once your child chooses a word, have him read it aloud before writing it in a tic-tac-toe square.

Tic-tac-toe can be played in a variety of places—while riding in the car, waiting at the doctor's office, sitting in a restaurant. All that's needed are paper and pencil. It's fun, simple, and quick! Make the game easy by selecting beginning consonants, or difficult by choosing diphthongs, diagraphs, or word endings. Your child, like my children, will probably ask to play game after game!

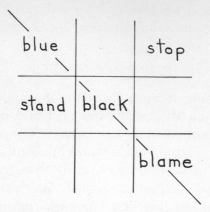

2. PHONICS MATCH

The object of this homemade card game is to collect four cards that have words with the same letter-sound combination. Use three-by-five cards to make the deck of twenty-four playing cards. Write a phonics essential, like **sh** or **ch,** and a word corresponding to the essential on each card, like **shake** or **chill.** If you are helping your child with diagraphs, your deck might have four cards each for **sh,**

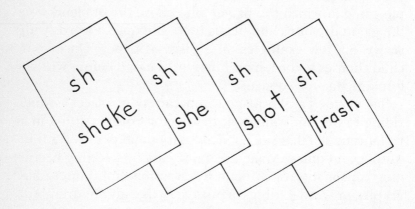

ch, th, and **wh,** like the cards for **sh** shown opposite—**she, shake, shot,** and **trash.**

Play Phonics Match by dealing six cards to each player and placing the rest facedown in a pile in the center of the table. Taking turns, players ask one another for a word with a particular phonics essential, "Do you have a word with **ai?**" If the answer is "yes," the **ai** card is given to the player who asked for it. The player who receives the card must then read the word before adding it to his hand. If no one has the card that's been requested, the player who asked for it draws from the pile on the table. When a player has a set of four cards matching the same essential, he puts the cards on the table and reads each word. The player with the most sets is the winner.

3. WORD-BUILDING MATRIX

This activity is particularly good for hard-to-learn vowels. Make a matrix by dividing a rectangle into nine squares. Write a vowel in the center square and put consonants in other squares. Have your child practice building words by adding letters to the beginning and end of the vowel. The illustration is an example of a matrix Timothy's mother

s	c	n
h	a	m
p	t	d

made for the short vowel sound of **a,** and the words six-year-old Timothy built with it.

This activity is challenging and mind-engaging, and can be enjoyed at home or almost anyplace else. It is quick, easy to play, and has gotten high marks from nearly all the children I have played it with!

4. SOUND SORT

This simple, easy-to-make activity is especially fun for younger children. Like many of the learning activities in this book, it has been used for many years in classrooms. This activity asks your child to sort pictures of objects according to the beginning, middle, or ending sound. When Richard was learning beginning consonant sounds, he

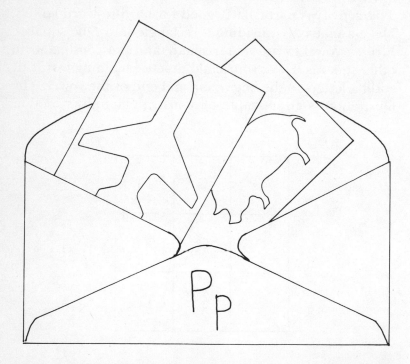

found the pictures of objects beginning with the sound of the letter **p,** as in the pictures of a **pig** and a **plane.**

Magazines are a good source of a variety of colorful pictures. Once you have cut out several pictures, put them in a large envelope for safekeeping. When it comes time to play Sound Sort, put the pictures on a table, and write the letter of the sound your child is listening for, say **Pp,** on a second envelope. Ask your child to put the pictures of things beginning with the sound of **Pp** in the corresponding envelope. There's no need to use new envelopes for this activity—write on the backs of envelopes you've received in the mail.

5. PHONICS CHAIN

If your child needs extra practice with beginning and ending consonants, blends and consonant diagraphs, Phonics Chain is a good activity that will be enjoyed by any age child. The object is to make a chain—similar to the one that results when domino tiles are arranged—by lining up words beginning or ending with like consonants. Suppose your child needs extra help with the consonant diagraphs **sh, ng,** and **ck.** First, make a set of cards (use three-by-five cards) with a word on each that begins or ends in **sh, ng,** and **ck—sheet, shack, sick, sing, shawl, rang, rack, luck,** and **fling,** for example. To play, put one card faceup and the rest facedown on a table. Now, you and your child pick up four cards each from the table. Taking turns, each player tries to find a word in his hand that begins or ends in the same consonants as the word on the table. A player who doesn't have a match draws a card from the pile on the table. The first person to play all of his or her cards wins the game.

The illustration below shows part of a game Kesha and her mother played. You can see here how the words lined up to make a chain.

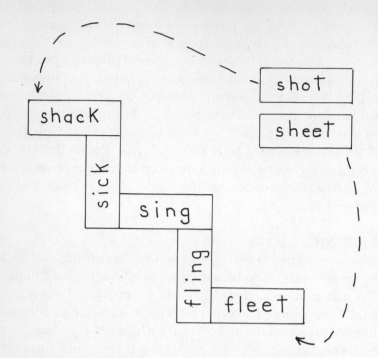

6. MYSTERY PICTURE

Mystery Picture works with any phonics essential; is easy to make; may appeal to younger children, say kindergarten through second grade; and is terrific for those times that call for a quiet activity. Here's what you do: Draw a large, simple picture on a blank sheet of paper, and divide the paper into sections. Put words that match a phonics essential in each section of the picture and words that do not show a phonics essential in other sections.

Your child discovers the mysterious picture by coloring the sections with words that match a phonics essential. When six-year-old Eric needed some practice with long vowel sounds, his mother asked him to color all the parts that have words with a long **i** vowel sound. This is the Mystery Picture Eric colored.

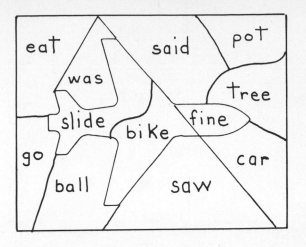

7. SOUND SLIDE

Many of the kindergarten, first-, and second-grade class-rooms as well as many of the classes for older remedial readers that I visit are equipped with some version of Sound Slide. To make a slide you'll need some stiff paper, preferably construction paper or tagboard. Cut a circle (or some other design) out of the paper and make two slits, as shown in the illustration. Now cut a long piece of paper, wide enough to slide through the slits. Write a letter-sound combination from one of the phonics essentials on the circle, and letters that will combine to make words on the long piece of paper. Your slide is finished.

Each time your child moves the long piece of paper through the slits, a different word appears. Two examples follow, one slide made by Monica's mother to teach blends, the other made by Ted's mother to teach word endings.

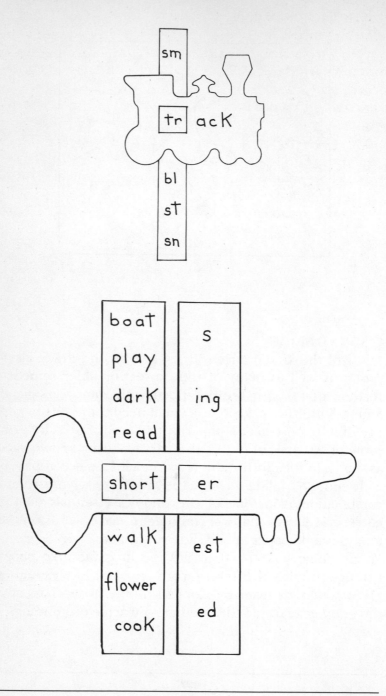

8. PHONICS PUZZLES

The aim of this activity is to create a word by putting the pieces of a puzzle together. Phonics Puzzles are challenging when the words are separated into several parts and easier when words are divided into only two parts. Begin by thinking of a word that is a good example of a phonics essential your child needs to learn. Write that word on a piece of paper and cut it apart. Your child puts the puzzle together by deciding how the letters combine to make the word. This simple yet challenging activity may appeal to younger children. Shown in the illustration are two Phonics Puzzles that were made by six-year-old Larry's mother, each demonstrating a different essential.

9. SOUND RACE

If your child loves to play board games, as mine does, Sound Race is sure to be a hit. If you have an old board game around the house—perhaps one with some missing pieces—you can use the old board to play this game. If you need to make a board, use the illustration as a starting point. Leave several squares blank and put directions in others—go backwards two spaces, or miss a turn, for example.

Once you have a board, make cards with words and numbers on them. Each word should be an example of a phonics essential. Each number tells the player how many spaces to move. To play, have each person draw a card, read the word on it, and move ahead as many spaces as the number on the card includes. If a player misses a word, he must put the card at the bottom of the pile. The illustration shows a game I made for my children. You can use the idea of a racetrack, as I did, or another theme that is of interest to your child.

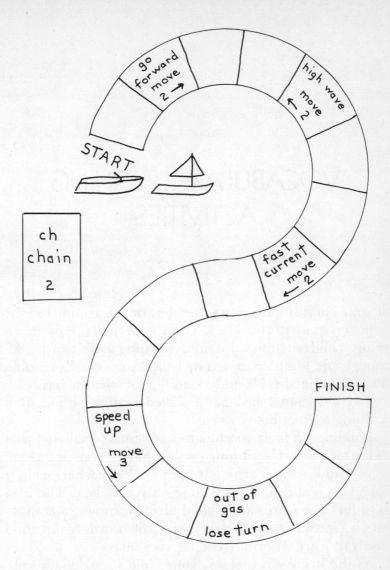

11

VOCABULARY LEARNING ACTIVITIES

If your child is a beginning reader, or has completed the primary grades, you know from experience how much effort children must put into learning new words. Although the ultimate means by which your child's reading ability is judged is his understanding of what he has read, your child cannot become a skilled reader without first learning a great many words.

Building up their vocabularies accounts for a large part of the total effort beginning readers put into reading. And, as we know, word learning is hard work. Teachers usually spend a great deal of class time on vocabulary. The idea is to link the words your child already knows in conversation (speaking vocabulary) with the words your child needs to learn in print (reading vocabulary).

As the bridge to literacy, your child's speaking vocabulary will exceed his reading vocabulary for a long time. Toward the end of the sixth grade, your child's reading vocabulary will begin to approach in size his speaking vocabulary. As a mature, adult reader, your child will know how to read many more words than he is able to use in conversation.

THE CONTEXT OF VOCABULARY

The jacket on my desktop dictionary boasts that there are nearly 160,000 words defined inside. A tried and true source of definitions and correct spelling, my dictionary gets a fair amount of use. Helpful as it is, though, the dictionary is not the first route I take to figure out the meaning of new words I come across in my reading.

Like all good readers, when I come to a new word, my initial reaction is to look to the surrounding words and the context of what I am reading for its meaning. Context is especially helpful because it throws light on the meaning of words. In books, the context is provided by the words in sentences. In the environment, the context is everything that normally appears within it, like swings on a playground or food in a grocery store.

Your child will seldom read words that do not appear in some sort of context—in sentences, on menus, in advertisements. Even the word **stop,** which we see all the time by itself, has a special sort of context in its red octagonal sign.

Long before my children could read books, and long before they went to school, they knew how to read words like McDonald's, Safeway (the grocery store), and Sears. But for my children and for other preschoolers, words like Safeway and Sears are only recognizable when they are seen in their customary environment. When I wrote out McDonald's on a piece of paper, my daughter, Susan, couldn't tell me what the word said. When we drove by McDonald's and she saw the word in the context of the golden arches, she knew where we were.

Now that my daughter is older, she reads many words without relying on clues like the red-white-and-blue circle around the word Pepsi. Yet the skill Susan used to link words within their environmental context remains a powerful tool. Now Susan links words within their reading context. Because context binds thoughts and words together in sentences, it provides readers with excellent clues to word meaning.

Sometimes the context offers so many clues that readers don't have to see the word to know what it is. For example: **By ten o'clock that night all the children were sound _____ in their beds.** On first reading you know the blank stands for **asleep.** You know because the context of the sentence leaves you no other feasible choice.

Just as you used context to decide that **asleep** was the missing word, your child uses context to make predictions about the words in the sentences he reads. But not all sentences have as many context clues as the example above. It depends on how a sentence is written.

Some sentences will ask your child to come up with several feasible words, as the next one does: **When I found John he was _____.** The only thing you know for sure from the context of this sentence is that the missing word indicates some sort of action or condition. John may have been asleep or eating, happy or jogging, angry or lost, etc.

Because the strength of context clues varies from sentence to sentence, good readers use a combination of context and phonics to identify new words. Context helps readers to figure out word meaning; phonics helps readers discover how an unknown word sounds. Used hand in hand, phonics and context are an unbeatable pair and a powerful word-learning tool.

RECOGNIZING
WORDS AUTOMATICALLY

Suppose your child hesitates for a few seconds while deciding what a word in a library book says. Is this kind of word recognition good enough? "Yes" would be the logical answer—after all, your child was correct. But being correct is only one part of what it takes to know a word. Your child has to be able to recognize a word so quickly, and with such a small amount of effort, that the whole process seems automatic. When recognition is immediate, it's as if the words in storybooks are on the tip of your child's tongue.

For skilled readers, recognition is so automatic that words seem to jump spontaneously into their minds. Automatic word recognition is something like turning on a lamp in a dark room. All you have to do is flip the switch that allows the current to flow—the light bulb glows and a previously dark room is now light. Too, just seeing words triggers recognition.

Have you ever caught yourself reading advertisements or newspaper headlines before you thought about what you were doing? I always read magazine covers when I'm standing in line at the supermarket—partly out of habit, partly from curiosity, and partly as a result of being a good reader amid a sea of words. This sort of spontaneous, automatic word recognition is what advertisers count on and what good readers do.

Recognizing words automatically takes very little attention, and attention is in limited supply. If you are listening to an editorial on the radio, you cannot write a letter at the same time. You can shift your attention back and forth, but you can't do both well simultaneously—each activity takes too much attention. But not all activities require a lot of conscious effort. Things we're accustomed to doing—driving the car, scrambling eggs, dialing the telephone—don't demand much, if any, conscious effort.

While beginning readers can afford to pay a fair amount of attention to word recognition, skilled readers cannot. Because stories for beginning readers don't often stray far from children's background experiences, comprehension does not take as much concentration as would be necessary to understand new information. Beginning readers can (and do) put great effort into word recognition.

The situation is different for older, more skilled readers. The materials that older children read are not as easily understood. Their reading matter covers a broad range of topics and introduces a variety of new ideas. Understanding this kind of material takes tremendous effort, and comprehension suffers when children concentrate too much on identifying individual words.

The goal of schoolteachers, and the aim of the learning activities in this chapter, is to increase the number of words your child recognizes automatically. The more words your child identifies quickly and accurately, the better he will read.

WHICH WORDS SHOULD YOU TEACH?

As busy parents, none of us have unlimited time. Even if we did, our children don't have unlimited staying power. And so we must choose which words to teach. My advice is to concentrate first on the words necessary for your child to be successful in the school reading program.

The words your child meets in the classroom are the words he must know in order to do assignments, read his schoolbooks, and answer comprehension questions. Your child's teacher, then, is the best resource for finding good words. The teacher knows which words are in your child's reading books, and which your child needs help remembering.

If your child is learning to read in a basal reading program, the teacher can give you a complete list of words your child will meet in the basal readers. Even if the school uses a whole-language approach, the teacher will be able to tell you which words in the library books your child is reading seem to be causing the greatest confusion.

By suggesting that you get a vocabulary list from the teacher, I don't mean to imply that words appearing outside of school reading materials are not worth learning. Words from all sorts of books your child might read for pleasure, words your child has a special interest in learning, and words from poems and songs have an important place and should also become part of your child's reading vocabulary. There is no need, nor is it desirable, to limit the words in the vocabulary learning activities to include only those on the school reading list. Think instead of the school list as a good starting point. Once your child is well into the school's list, go beyond it by helping your child to learn any other words he wishes to include in his vocabulary. It's a matter of how much emphasis you place on the words on your child's school list and how much you place on words from other sources.

If your child is climbing the reading pyramid on schedule, he should be reading on or above grade level. In this case, include some words from the school's list but spend extra time helping your child to learn words beyond the scope of the reading program. You'll be offering your child a chance for enrichment, a chance to extend his reading vocabulary, a chance that he might not have in the classroom.

It's a different story if your child is behind in reading. In this case, the bulk of the words should be those your child is expected to learn in school. My experience with below-average readers has been that targeting words in the school reading program pays off in a big way. When a child is behind, the immediate objective is to get that child back on track, as quickly as possible. Helping your child to learn the words in his school books is an important step in the right direction.

Don't worry about your child learning so many words at home that he will be bored in school. If he's behind in reading and goes to school knowing some of the words that will appear in his school books, that's just what you want. Knowing those words builds self-confidence, something your child is probably lacking. I would much rather have a self-confident youngster tell me that he "already knows that word" than have a child shy away from reading, believing he will not recognize the words in his books.

If, for whatever reason, you are not able to get a vocabulary list from your child's teacher, there are other resources you can tap. Over the years, experts have put together lists of words recommended for children in the elementary grades. The Dolch List (56) is perhaps the best known. The Dolch List is a handy list to have, especially if your child is in the primary grades. The 220 words on the list account for up to 76 percent of the words used in first-grade books, 69 percent of the words in second-grade books, and over 62 percent of the words used in third-grade books (73).

You can probably get a copy of Dolch's 220 words from your child's teacher, or consult the note at the end of the book to order one. The Dolch List is, without question, the list most widely used in the early grades. Because the words on the list appear with such great frequency in children's books and because many of these words are rather difficult to learn, teachers in classrooms and in reading clinics make sure children recognize the words automatically.

One of the first things we do in our university reading clinic is find out if the children who come in can read the words authors use frequently. Often we'll ask children to read words from the Dolch List, and we routinely find poor readers who do not know these words. When we asked Claudia, a third-grader with poor reading skills, to read the words on the Dolch List, she knew fewer than half. She read **mother** as **matter, than** instead of **that,** and **again** for **always.** Because Claudia kept coming across these words in her textbooks and storybooks, her ability to read was severely hampered.

When children like Claudia routinely struggle with even the most basic words in their storybooks, reading offers little satisfaction and may leave them with a sense of failure and frustration. Stumbling over frequently used words can be debilitating to the point that the whole reading process breaks down—comprehension is impossible and reading becomes a chore. While we worked on many reading abilities with Claudia, teaching her the basic words in her reading books was one of our top priorities, and placing a high priority on teaching her those high-frequency words paid off. As Claudia learned to read more and more of the words, her self-confidence grew, her reading comprehension improved, and she went on to build a solid reading vocabulary.

Another good source of commonly used words is the list of three hundred "Instant Words" compiled by Edward Fry (74). Fry's list has the advantage of including words which comprise approximately 65 percent of the words read by children and adults. The authors of textbooks, newspaper and magazine articles, brochures, and so forth use the words on Fry's list with such frequency that the first ten words account for approximately 24 percent of all printed English words, the first one hundred for 50 percent of such words. If you want to obtain a copy of Fry's list, your child's teacher is the person to consult. If she doesn't have one, you can locate a copy using the information in Note 74.

LONG WORDS OR SHORT WORDS— WHICH ARE EASIEST TO LEARN?

No one would question that it takes practice to build up a storehouse of words. The question is, how much practice?

Should your child know a word the second time he sees it, the tenth time, the twenty-fifth time?

Unfortunately, there isn't a specific amount of practice that will guarantee automatic recognition. Your child will learn some words the first few times he sees them; other words will take many more repetitions. While I can't predict exactly how many times your child will need to see a word before he knows it, I can offer some insights into the conditions that influence how quickly your child learns.

As a general rule, long words are more easily remembered than short words. At first this seems backwards— long words should take more effort to learn because they have a lot of letters; short words should be easy because they have fewer. But in reality, it is the length and shape of long words that make them easier to learn. Learning a word like **telephone** is easy because its very shape separates it from most other words. Combine that unique shape with the **ph** that comes in the middle, and there isn't much chance that your child will confuse **telephone** with other words. Words like **telephone, Christmas, hippopotamus,** and **bicycle** are unique, and your child will likely learn them with ease.

Providing a sharp contrast to the distinct appearance of long words, short words tend to be of similar lengths and shapes. Certain short words are notorious; **went** and **want, was** and **saw, than** and **then, some** and **same** are among the harder-to-learn short words. In addition to their similarity in length and shape, words like **when-where** and **that-than** share many of the same letters. The more words look like one another, the fewer their distinguishing characteristics and the harder they are to learn. Even with good sentence context, your child may find words like these to be a stumbling block.

Because short, similar-looking words are easily confused, I wasn't surprised when first-grade Juan misread **was** for **saw** in the sentence, "The boy saw his baseball fly into the air." Being a good reader, Juan recognized his mistake and quickly corrected the error. In Juan's case, misreading **was** for **saw** wasn't a sign of reading difficulty; short words like **was** and **saw** are so troublesome that it takes some children up through second grade to read them error-free.

If long words are easier to learn, why not help your child learn them first and work on short words later when your child has more reading experience? Here is the trouble: those short, hard-to-learn words also happen to be the words used by authors again and again in children's books. This makes it imperative that your child learn the more challenging short words right away even if it requires some extra effort.

Another thing that makes a word easy or hard to learn is how readily it creates a picture in your child's mind. Have you ever seen a **cat?** Can you picture **jumping** or **climbing?** How about **was** and **for?** Do **was** and **for** bring any images to mind? While **cat** and **jumping** are easy for your child to picture, **was** doesn't call up any mental image.

Words like **cat** and **jump** have a built-in bridge to memory, a bridge of pictures and images that solidly anchor words in your child's mind. Words that aren't related to a specific mental image are going to be more difficult for your child to learn to read.

Don't worry if your child needs extra practice with words that aren't connected with solid mental images. This is perfectly natural. By using the learning suggestions in this chapter, your child will get enough practice to recognize automatically all the words necessary to be a good reader, whatever curious characteristics the words may have.

LEARNING WORDS
WITH THE LOOK-SAY METHOD

Look-say, sometimes called the sight method, has been around since people first began to write. When one looks at drawings of animals on the walls of caves, it seems that ancient people connected each drawing with a complete spoken word, or perhaps even a whole concept. The picture of an antelope probably stood for the spoken word, as did the drawings of other animals, celestial bodies, and so forth. Look-say operates on the same basic idea of connecting a whole written word with a whole spoken word. Look-say comes naturally to parents, in part because it's easy to use, but also because of the kinds of questions children ask. You've probably used look-say before, but may not know it.

When my son, Brian, became interested in words, he began to ask lots of questions about words wherever he saw them—on signs, in books, printed on his toys. Brian would point to words and ask me what they said. He asked countless questions: "Mom, what does that say?" pointing to the word **closed** on the door of the bagel shop. Sometimes he would spell, asking, "What does **c-l-o-s-e-d** say?" I always answered with the whole word—**closed.** That's look-say.

If look-say plays an important role in the way we answer our children's questions at home, it is no less important for teaching reading in your child's classroom. One major reason teachers use look-say is because some words in our language cannot be sounded out using phonics. In the case of words that don't work with phonics, look-say is the only available route to word learning.

Many of the most frequently used words in English do not sound the way they are spelled. Words like **one, here,** and **only** cannot be pronounced with phonics, yet they appear in print often. Taking a closer look at the word

one, we see that the problem lies with the sound of the letter **o.** Rather than sounding like the **o** in **tone,** as it should with a final **e,** the **o** in **one** corresponds to the sound at the beginning of **water.** No matter how hard your child tries to use phonics to figure out the word **one,** he will never come up with a reasonable approximation of how this word sounds. It's much easier to remember the whole written word.

What we want, then, is to have our children strike a reasonable balance between memorizing words with look-say and relying on phonics to sound out words. Given that some words work with phonics and others do not, both teaching methods have an important place in your child's classroom and in your home learning activities.

LEARNING ACTIVITIES

Of the three areas covered in this book (phonics, vocabulary, and comprehension), your child is likely to make the quickest, most visible gains in vocabulary. There are ten vocabulary learning activities, each of which is aimed at helping your child to read more and more words automatically. As always, you want the best combined fit of learning activities and your child's capabilities. To this end, use your knowledge of your child's preferences as the basis for changing the learning activities in any way you feel might be helpful.

Perhaps you are wondering how many words your child should learn at once. My recommendation is to begin with no more than five new words at a time, particularly if your child is in the first grade, or is having difficulty learning to read. Beginning with five or fewer words ensures success since younger children do not have to hold so many different words in memory. If your child is a second-grader or older, he may feel comfortable working on more than five new words at once. Above all, it is crucial that your child have a sense of accomplishment, something that is a natural outgrowth of knowing he is doing well.

Sometimes when we get very young children or less-skilled readers in the university reading clinic, we teach only two or three new words at a time. A few years ago, I spent several months working with a little boy, Elroy, who learned just one new word at a time. A third-grader, Elroy couldn't even name the twenty-six letters of the alphabet. Trying to teach him a number of different words at once was more than confusing—it was useless. After Elroy had learned approximately fifty words, he began to feel a real sense of accomplishment. For the first time Elroy could read very easy books. Only then was he comfortable learning more than one word at a time.

Your child, like Elroy, may be more comfortable learning one or two words at a time. Or perhaps your child can easily handle more than five words at once. It isn't how many words your child learns at one time, it's the way your child feels about his ability to learn them that counts. It is far more productive for your child to learn a few words each week, learn them well, and feel good about his ability than it is to include so many words in the learning activities that your child becomes confused and remembers only partially.

1. WORD HUNT

Word Hunt is a short, fun activity that appeals to children of all ages. I've used it for years with youngsters who need an extra boost to help them remember words. Begin by writing several words on a sheet of paper and telling your child he is going on a word hunt. Then give your child a newspaper or magazine; ask him to hunt for the words and circle them. Once your child has circled all the words he can find, count how many times he found each one. Give your child extra practice by asking him to read the words he finds.

2. HIDDEN WORDS

As a quick review, this game is particularly good for children who are in the second grade or older. If your child recognizes a word some of the time, but not all of the time, Hidden Words is a helpful prescription. Begin by writing a word on a blank sheet of paper. Write several extra letters in front and behind the word. Your child's job is to find the hidden word, circle it, and read it aloud. To give a sense of how Hidden Words works, I've included examples of activities I collected from Jennifer's mother. When Jennifer needed help with the words **celebrate** and **pottery,** her mother made the Hidden Words puzzles below.

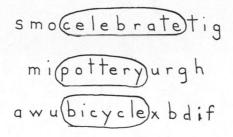

3. MOUSE AND CHEESE

This is my seven-year-old's favorite game, and a favorite of older elementary-age children as well. You'll probably recognize this activity as a version of the game Hangman—the objectives of the games are similar—without the implication of violence that may be associated with Hangman. Think of a word your child needs to practice. Now make a blank space at the bottom of a sheet of paper for each letter in the word and draw a large piece of cheese. Have your child try to guess the word one letter at a time. Write each correctly guessed letter in its space at the bottom of the page; for each incorrect letter guessed draw one part of the mouse. The game ends when your child spells the entire word or makes enough mistakes so that the mouse is completely drawn. If your child guesses the word, the cheese goes uneaten. But if your child misses the word, the fully drawn mouse can eat the cheese.

You can make the game easier by giving your child a brief definition of the word he is trying to guess. Sometimes we switch places; my daughter thinks of the mystery word and I do the guessing. Either way, Mouse and Cheese is a fast, fun learning game that will enhance your child's reading vocabulary. The illustration below shows a game my daughter and I played recently.

4. MAZES

Mazes are a long-standing favorite and an activity your child is sure to enjoy. Like Hidden Words, mazes are best used with words your child knows but needs to practice, rather than with words being learned for the first time. As shown in the following illustration, mazes are made up of boxes, each with a letter inside. Words are hidden in the maze; your child must find and circle them. It is extremely important to make the words in your mazes read in the same direction as they do in books, horizontally and from left to right. One of the mazes seven-year-old Cassia's mother made looked like the following illustration.

You can buy activity books with maze-type word puzzles, but be careful: most of the mazes in these books arrange

s	a	t	f	z
y	h	o	l	e
b	a	l	l	g
g	i	r	l	f
w	h	i	t	a

words in all sorts of directions—from right to left (the wrong way for reading), top to bottom, diagonally, and backwards. Finding words written in different directions can be a great deal of fun, but if your child is having problems remembering the words on the page, trying to find words written in strange ways is more confusing than helpful.

5. SEARCH AND MATCH

This is a memory game. It is an especially good activity for more than one person, so invite other family members to join in. After deciding which words you want to include in the game, write a word on three separate three-by-five cards—include at least ten words in the game. When the cards are ready, divide the deck into two piles. One pile will have only one card for each word; the other has two cards for each word. Scramble the pile that has two cards for each word and place the cards facedown in five rows on a table (rows will have four cards each). Now put the pile with one card for each word facedown on the table and turn the top card faceup.

To play Search and Match, your child must read the word on the faceup card and find matches by remembering which card in which row, when turned faceup, has the same word written on it. Each time your child finds a match and reads it aloud, he gets to keep the cards. The person who has the most matches wins.

When Allen was learning high-frequency words like **car, hit, go,** and **here,** he played Search and Match with his mother. The drawing shows one of their games.

6. BINGO

Bingo is another old standby, a favorite among children of any age, and part of the repertoire of every elementary teacher I know. Play bingo with your child just as you would ordinarily play the game, but substitute words for letters and numbers. Instead of having B4 or G15 on your bingo card, write words like **won't** and **where.** I've included an example to help you visualize what a homemade bingo card should look like.

If you make a number of different bingo cards with a variety of combinations, everyone in the family can play.

won't	stop	shoe	hit
fast	when	pan	hat
where	car	was	get
fall	saw	why	got

It's a good game for after dinner and a great alternative to watching television. If you have younger children at home, include them, too. Perhaps your older, school-age child would like to help a younger sister or brother find the right words on the bingo card.

7. HIGH STAKES

High Stakes is a homemade card game where the object is to gather the most points by reading words on three-by-five cards. Make a High Stakes deck by writing one word per three-by-five card along with the number of points the word is worth; include at least twenty cards in the deck. Hard-to-read words are worth more points, easy words fewer points. Since **where** is harder to remember than **suitcase,** you might make **where** worth five points and **suitcase** worth only two points.

Play High Stakes by placing the cards facedown in a stack on the table. Players take turns drawing cards and reading the words on them. Every time a word is read correctly, the player keeps the card, adding the points to his total score. If your child is in charge of keeping score, the practice with addition is an added benefit! The illustration below is an example of the cards Taylor's mother made.

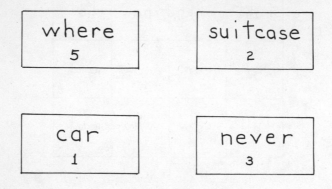

8. TWO CHOICES

As an activity for keeping words in context, Two Choices has been popular in classrooms for a long time. While educators have come up with different variations, the version I have found easiest to use at home is the one described here.

Find a few sentences from a library book your child has brought home, or make up several yourself. Now delete one or two words from each sentence. If a sentence is long, say over eight words in length, you may wish to delete two words. With shorter sentences, delete only one word. Draw a line where the missing word should be, and write two choices below the line. Your child will read the sentence and decide which word is the right choice.

Here are two examples of sentences mothers have used with their children at home. One was used with first-grade Kory; the other with fourth-grade Simone. Kory's sentence looked like this:

It is _____ cold to play outside today.
 too two

Simone's sentence was harder:

The spider spun his web _____ the porch light.
 beside before

9. SENTENCE MIX-UP

Like Two Choices, Sentence Mix-up keeps words in context. Play this game by thinking of a sentence. Write each word separately on a three-by-five card and scramble the cards; now ask your child to arrange the words to make a sentence. Here is one of the mixed-up sentences ten-year-old Paul figured out: **hit John the game home run last during Saturday a.** The proper sequence is: **John hit a home run during the game last Saturday.**

Because Paul is a fifth-grader, the sentence his mother chose was rather long. For younger children, use three or four words to begin and then build up to longer, more complex sentences.

10. CLASSIFYING

Classifying words is a terrific way to help your child learn their definitions and to teach word recognition at the same time. First, decide on several categories your child is familiar with, like animals, transportation, food, etc. Use at least two categories each time you play, more if you like. Write words that are examples of each category on three-by-five cards.

To classify words, your child sorts them by placing each word under the correct category. Six-year-old Henry especially liked this activity, and I have included an example of one of the classifying activities he enjoyed.

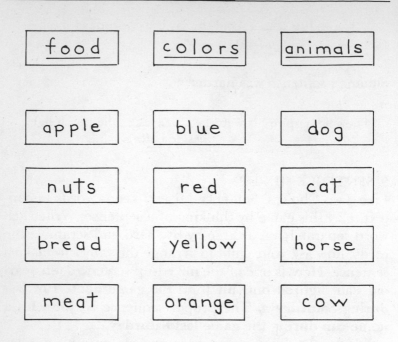

A word about flash cards. Flash cards can be helpful, provided you use them with caution. Set aside the idea of drill and practice—use flash cards creatively. It's fun to find flash cards with words that rhyme, are opposites, that describe an action (go, come, jump), begin with the same letter, end with the same letter, and so forth. The possibilities for using flash cards are almost endless.

As a reminder of how many words your child has learned, reading flash cards can be highly motivating. To emphasize the number of words your child is learning, sort flash cards into two piles: one group of words that are "automatic" and the other, a group of words that fall into a "not sure yet" category. As your child learns more words, the number of cards in the "automatic" pile grows, and with it your child's self-confidence.

From time to time, my daughter likes to read flash cards, perhaps because the stack of words she knows is so impressive. One Saturday afternoon Susan found a big stack of old flash cards in a drawer we were cleaning. She asked her father to show her the cards, which he agreed to do. Having spent quite some time in the messy drawer, the cards weren't all right side up. Susan's dad didn't notice though; when I went into the next room, there was Susan with a large pile of cards beside her and her father showing her the cards, most of them upside down. Susan knew them anyway! Perhaps the lesson here is that children who know words "automatically" can recognize them written in almost any direction, and adults need to be watchful of the way flash cards are held!

12

COMPREHENSION LEARNING ACTIVITIES

Your child may pick up a book and read it for a variety of different reasons—perhaps he wants to learn about space travel, or needs some information to write a report, or possibly he is captured by an exciting story. Whatever the reason for reading, comprehension hinges on the manner in which your child connects his background experiences to the topic he is reading about.

Because each person brings different background experiences to reading, no two come away with identical interpretations of something they've both read. Newspaper articles are a good example of how background knowledge and experience influence reading comprehension. Recently our local paper published a tribute to a retiring legislator. Reactions to the editorial from readers ranged from enthusiastic and supportive to downright hostile. The written words were the same; what colored the different readers' perceptions were their political views.

Comprehension is a well-traveled two-way street between reader and author. The author's words trigger thoughts in your child's mind in one direction. Your child uses his background knowledge from the other direction to make sense out of ideas the author has written about. For example, the words on the menu in my favorite Mexican restaurant don't have any meaning unless I know the English translation. Meaning was already in the mind of the chef who wrote *arroz con pollo* on the menu, and meaning must also be in my mind if I am to understand that the chef is serving chicken with rice.

At the heart of good reading is an ability to use this two-way street that allows your child to read the Sunday comics one minute, and be able to understand his social studies textbook the next. This is the kind of comprehension elementary school reading programs work toward, and the sort of comprehension that is the focus of this chapter.

THINKING ABOUT MEANING

First and foremost, children with good comprehension consider the meaning of the words in their storybooks and textbooks. By emphasizing the importance of thinking, I do not wish to overlook the contribution of phonics and vocabulary. There is no question that comprehension depends on knowing the words—something that is accomplished only by using phonics and remembering words with look-say. Yet phonics and vocabulary do not necessarily guarantee good reading comprehension. Children can know a great deal about phonics and vocabulary and still have poor comprehension. Thomas was just such a child.

The first time he came to our university reading clinic, we asked Thomas to read a short passage aloud. From start to finish, Thomas read with confidence and expression. Judging from all outward signs, Thomas should have had a very good understanding of what he was reading. After listening to Thomas's error-free reading, the university student working with him was convinced that he had no reading problems. She wanted to know why a good reader like Thomas would come to a remedial reading clinic.

Had she asked Thomas any comprehension questions, I wondered? No, she had not. Thomas's oral reading sounded so good that it seemed logical that he had understood what he read. Yet this was not the case. Out of ten comprehension questions, Thomas could answer only two. Thomas was pronouncing the words, but he wasn't thinking about their meaning.

A product of thinking, reading comprehension relies on many different reasoning skills—knowing how to find information, to follow directions, and to determine cause and effect, to name a few. These are the kinds of skills we taught Thomas and things your child needs to learn, too.

WHAT YOUR CHILD NEEDS TO KNOW

Unlike phonics, about which teachers continue to debate the issues, there is some agreement on what to teach when it comes to comprehension. As a consequence, virtually all elementary school reading programs teach the same comprehension abilities. Many elementary reading programs focus on teaching separate comprehension abilities, like following directions, recognizing characters' emotions, and identifying propaganda techniques. However, teaching practice differs from what experts tell us about the way children understand storybooks and textbooks.

Experts believe that comprehension is a thinking process that cannot be separated into parts. Given the view of these experts, you may be wondering why schools continue to teach separate comprehension abilities. The truth is that no one yet has come up with a better method. Over the years, teachers have found that when specific comprehension abilities were taught, children's reading comprehension improved. These are the same comprehension abilities your child learns in school and the abilities I will discuss in this chapter.

Finding the main idea. Understanding any sort of reading material hinges on recognizing the main idea, or central point, that the author is trying to make. A passage beginning with "Whales are mammals who live in the ocean" is clearly going to focus on whales and their lives as ocean-going mammals. Few readers will be in the dark about the point being made by the author.

When it comes to physically writing down the main idea, there are three basic patterns used by authors: describing the main idea in a sentence like the one about whales is the most straightforward way an author has of communicating to your child the central point. If the author who wrote about whales put the main idea in the first sentence and followed it with supporting facts and details (i.e., the size of whales, their life span and eating habits), the pattern would look something like this:

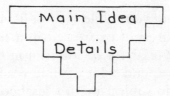

Newspapers generally use this sort of pattern because it lets readers know from the very start what the article is going to be about, and gives its readers specific facts and details about the topic.

The second pattern works in the opposite direction. Rather than including the main idea in the first sentence, the author gives his readers the gist of the passage in the last sentence. The pattern will look something like this:

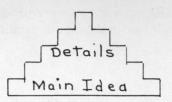

Sometimes authors do not put the main idea in a single sentence. Instead, they will imply the gist of what follows, leaving your child to cull the main idea from it on his own. Paragraphs or passages following this third pattern look like the rectangle in the drawing.

> Mixture of
> facts and ideas

When authors use the third pattern, your child must use abstract thinking skills to read between the lines for the main idea.

The place where your child is most likely to come across main ideas that are not expressed in a single sentence is in subject-matter textbooks. Children in the fourth, fifth, and sixth grades spend a lot of time reading this kind of book. Not only do subject-matter textbooks often use the third pattern, but they are chock-full of facts, details, ideas, and concepts.

No child, however bright, can remember everything in a health book, a social studies book, or a science book. Knowing the main idea puts your child in the position of being able to decide what information in the textbook is relevant to the central topic and what information is not. Once the essential information is separated from the superfluous, your child can concentrate on remembering and understanding the things that are most closely related to the author's subject matter.

Because poor readers can't distinguish which information is essential to an understanding of the topic, they become bogged down with too many loose facts and end up missing the author's point. I remember asking Troy, a fifth-grader, to read a passage about treehoppers—tiny green and brown insects on trees and bushes. Troy was having some difficulty understanding his subject-matter textbooks, but it didn't take long to discover the source of his trouble. When I asked Troy what the passage was about, he told me it might have had something to do with treehoppers laying eggs, but he wasn't sure. While egg laying *was* mentioned, the author's purpose was to clearly describe treehoppers—what they look like, where they live, how they eat, etc. Troy had missed the main point and, in so doing, failed to fully understand the passage.

Had he been taking a comprehension test, Troy would have received a very low score. Had he been trying to learn about treehoppers, he would have gained little, if any, useful information. In contrast to children like Troy, good readers look for the main idea and set about to remember the facts and details that serve to support the author's central theme.

Remembering facts and details. Suppose your child was asked to read the same passage about treehoppers that Troy read. In order to understand the passage, your child must decide what is of importance and then remember that information. Use the **4 W** questions—**who, what, where,** and **when**—to help your child recall that information. Because they constitute the most widespread method for teaching children how to remember facts and details, your child is bound to learn about the **4 W** questions in school. Teachers have used the technique for many years, and it continues to be a staple for teaching comprehension.

Rather than reading aimlessly through the passage on treehoppers as poor readers like Troy often do, the **4 W** questions cause your child's attention to be focused on relevant, useful information. Using the passage about treehoppers as an example, your child could read to find out **what** treehoppers look like, **where** treehoppers live, and **when** they lay eggs. The **who** question isn't asked—had the passage discussed a scientist, a question about **who** could be included.

It's been my experience that children learn to remember facts and details relatively easily, provided they have some grasp of the main idea. One reason that facts and details are easy to recall is that children can often match the words in the questions you ask with the words in the sentences of their books. If you ask your child "When do treehoppers' eggs hatch?" he can show you exactly where the author explains that "Eggs hatch in the spring." By combining the **4 W** questions with the other learning activities in this chapter, you'll come away with a solid, proven means for developing comprehension abilities and will have every reason to believe that your child will be successful.

Following directions. To my way of thinking, any child who can cope with the pace and demands of modern family life is more than capable of learning to follow directions, even complex multi-step directions. Teachers agree because nearly every activity in school requires that your child be able to follow directions.

Most directions are written clearly enough that readers can follow them without too much effort, but this certainly isn't always the case. For his last birthday, my son got a present with such confusing directions that it took several tries, not to mention a great deal of frustration, before the toy was properly assembled. Whether they are easy or difficult to follow, we can't afford to misunderstand the directions that come with things like medicine bottles, fire extinguishers, recipes, and household appliances.

Your child will begin learning to read directions in first grade and will continue to work on the skill well beyond the time he has reached the last tier of the elementary school reading pyramid. Teachers usually begin with one-step directions. Then, when children's reading ability improves, teachers will introduce more complex, multi-step directions.

Following directions is not as simple as remembering facts and details. Even older children need a lot of practice. Sometimes difficulty mastering this ability spills over into everyday school work with predictably disastrous results.

I worked with one little boy, Frederick, who spent two-thirds of his fourth-grade year without ever getting his assignments straight. He was continually turning to the wrong page in his textbooks, answering the wrong questions, and giving his teacher papers that were both incorrect and confusing. Frederick couldn't make sense out of even the most basic directions.

One of his problems was that Frederick didn't listen when his teacher told the class what to do. A second was that Frederick hadn't developed sufficient ability at following instructions to understand what he was supposed to do when he read directions on his own. After some time, Frederick's school work was suffering to the point that he began to fall behind his classmates. His teacher spent a good many extra hours working with Frederick on following directions. Once he gained some competence reading and understanding directions, Frederick's class work improved immensely as did his overall achievement in school.

Following directions is such an integral part of doing well in school that your child cannot afford to have difficulty with this ability. I believe this so fully that one of the questions I ask during parent-teacher conferences is how well the children are able to follow directions. (This is mentioned in Chapter 5.) If you suspect that your child needs more practice following directions, there are two excellent activities explained in this chapter.

Use the learning activities in this chapter, but do not overlook the rich opportunities that are part of your everyday family routine as a source for extra practice. The box of instant pudding has short, easy-to-follow directions. So do soup cans. Everyone loves popcorn; have your child read and follow the directions on a container of popcorn. Many toys have directions that your child can follow; try those inexpensive balsa wood airplanes that need to be put together, or kites and easy models. These are but a few suggestions—you'll think of many more!

Recognizing correct order. If your child can retell stories from his library books keeping the sequence of events, characters, relationships, and actions straight, he has a good sense of correct order. If your child becomes confused, loses track of the action, forgets about important relationships, and mixes up characters and events, he needs help with this skill.

Should your child have any difficulty recognizing correct order, he is bound to have problems following directions. Part of following directions is being able to understand that each step is important and must be followed in the right sequence. Since recognizing correct order and following directions are related, this is a good chance to double up on your teaching objectives. Any activity aimed at teaching your child how to follow directions is also going to help him figure out correct order, provided you point out the words that signal the sequence of events.

Authors often use certain words to signal proper order. As a consequence, it is definitely worth helping your child learn to pay attention to signal words like **first, second, last, now, before, next, then,** and **after.** If you have been reading aloud to your child, detecting correct order in storybooks is probably something your child has already learned a bit about. What your child needs now is to learn how to apply the ability to reading. The learning activities in this chapter will help to sharpen that ability.

Determining cause and effect. Determining cause and effect depends upon knowing the main idea, important facts and details, and correct order. Even the youngest readers need to have some sense of cause and effect in order to understand the stories they read. Further, by fourth grade your child should have developed this ability far beyond understanding cause and effect in simple stories.

Of all the reading your fourth-, fifth-, or sixth-grader does in school, the social studies and science books top the list for the number of explanations of cause-and-effect relationships that they contain. A science book that states "Temperatures above thirty-two degrees cause ice and snow to melt" clearly sets forth a cause-and-effect relationship. Plainly stated cause-and-effect relationships like this one should pose few problems for your child.

But not all textbooks make such clear statements and not all cause-and-effect relationships are that simple. Your child is bound to come across something more like this: "Because she was having a hard time breathing, Mrs. Jones didn't go outside all day. Looking out the window, she could see a thick haze covering the city. Up in the mountains a forest fire burned, moving rapidly over the hills, consuming trees, bushes, and any wildlife not fast enough to escape the heat of its flames."

The author doesn't directly define cause and effect, nor does the author list a single set of actions and reactions. The passage describes a chain of events in which some actions trigger other events, which in turn result in still other consequences. Learning to determine cause and effect in this kind of passage takes a great deal of practice.

My suggestion is to help your child learn cause and effect with the help of another **W** question—**why. Why** do ice and snow melt? **Why** did Mrs. Jones have a hard time breathing? **Why** was the air thick with haze? By answering these questions, your child is automatically drawn to the causes—temperatures above thirty-two degrees, poor air quality, and a forest fire in the mountains.

My second suggestion is to help your child pay attention to signal words. **Because, if, due to, when, since, therefore, as a result of, as a consequence, unless, hence, in order that, for, so, so that, as,** and **then** all act as reliable indications of the cause-and-effect relationship. Your fourth-grader should be able to use some, but probably not all, of these signal words. As a sixth-grader, your child should be using every one. Once your child is able to determine cause-and-effect relationships, he is ready to look beyond what the author has written, to read between the lines.

Reading critically. Our society puts a high value on the strength of written words. Ask anyone about believability and you're likely to hear "I read it in the newspaper" or "So-and-so says that in her book." Authors write for many reasons—to entertain their readers, to inform a particular audience, to teach a skill, to express an opinion or philosophy. With so many reasons for writing, it is imperative that your child learn to read critically.

Most elementary school reading programs recognize this and begin teaching critical reading in the first grade. In the early elementary years, your child learns to identify characters' emotions and to differentiate between fantasy and reality. For example, upon reading a story about children who encounter creatures from outer space, younger readers might be asked to explain how the children in the story might feel about their encounter and whether the story was true or make-believe.

As he matures and his abstract reasoning ability becomes

better developed, the school reading program teaches your child to separate fact from opinion, to detect missing information in articles and reports, to appreciate innuendo and multiple meanings, and to recognize propaganda and identify bias. Recently, I observed a sixth-grade teacher use an editorial from the newspaper to teach a lesson on critical reading. She asked her students to read the editorial and identify bias in sentences like this: "As mayor of the city of Hometown, John Doe has done little to promote growth and prosperity." The homework assigned to the students involved reading an editorial, determining the author's point of view, and identifying two examples of bias. Other activities used in the classroom included underlining words indicative of the use of propaganda, and listing facts and opinions. Without question, these abilities are core requirements for being a fully functioning, literate adult.

Because most kinds of critical reading depend on abstract thinking skills that children beyond age eight are still developing, it is reasonable to expect better and better critical reading of your child as he grows older. Yet the National Assessment of Educational Progress (NAEP) does not show a trend toward improvement. A nationwide testing program aimed at determining how well our children are developing in basic skills, the NAEP is the best information we have about reading achievement. Its reports tell us that, in recent years, fourth-graders have improved their understanding of information that is specifically stated in passages—they may be able to recall, for example, that John Doe is the mayor of Hometown. While this finding is reassuring, the NAEP reports on the comprehension of older children are not as encouraging. Older children, who should have good abstract thinking skills, demonstrate second-rate comprehension skills when it comes to understanding anything beyond surface-level information. This is especially alarming since knowing how to read critically is the sort of upper-level reading ability on which we rely to keep our democratic system in order and remain competitive in world markets.

Whatever the cause of this lackluster performance nationwide, your child need not fall into this group. When it comes to differentiating between fact and opinion, help your older child to learn that facts can be verified, but that opinions cannot. If an author writes that Phoenix is the capital of Arizona, your child can easily check this out in the encyclopedia. On the other hand, the statement that Phoenix is among the most beautiful cities in the Southwest cannot be verified. It is an opinion. Most of the time, authors combine facts with their opinions, making it challenging for readers to separate one from the other. Authors who mix fact and opinion are often trying to sway a reader in his views on a topic. Your child needs to be aware of some of the persuasive techniques authors employ, particularly propaganda techniques.

Every time I think of propaganda I picture a foreign government trying furtively to sway American public opinion. But this isn't an accurate perception. Even the youngest child is constantly being exposed to propaganda techniques. When an ad campaign against drug abuse convinces your child to say "No," propaganda is helpful. When an ad encourages your child to do something poor for his health, like eat too much sugar, propaganda is harmful. It is not the techniques of propaganda that are worrisome so much as the purposes that these techniques serve.

The elementary school reading program will teach older readers how to recognize seven propaganda techniques. These techniques are relatively simple to identify—they are used to a large degree in television advertising—and knowledge of them can greatly improve your child's reading ability as well as his ability to make thoughtful consumer decisions. When a commercial on television shows a woman in a nurse's uniform speaking on behalf of a certain medication, describes a product as "a revolutionary innovation," or informs viewers that over 90 percent of people buy a certain product, advertisers are using the propaganda techniques your older child will learn to recognize. These techniques include:

- **Name calling**—the use of disagreeable terms to create negative impressions, such as "the stingy man" or "the inefficient business."
- **Glittering generalities**—an attempt to persuade an audience by the use of vague overstatements, like "oven-fresh bread."
- **Plain folks**—a technique in which someone who is well-known, frequently a political candidate or performer, is made to look like your next-door neighbor.
- **Transfer**—the association of some respected symbol or organization with something else; for example, the use of a flag as a backdrop for a bicycle ad.
- **Testimonial**—like transfer, only here a famous person endorses a product, organization, or idea.
- **Bandwagon**—the "everyone is doing it" attempt to tap into your child's desire to be like his friends.
- **Card stacking**—deliberately omitting important information so that a rosy picture (usually one side of the story) is presented.

I have found that the easiest way to help children to recognize these techniques is to begin with advertising—television, newspaper, and magazine ads all offer rich sources for identifying techniques. Ask your child which techniques are used and whether he is going to let himself be influenced. When he becomes skilled at recognizing propaganda in advertising, ask him to answer the same questions about the material he reads. In some instances your child's answer will be "yes," he believes that the advertiser or author has a credible position, in others "no."

But in every instance, your child will be using his good critical reading ability to make a thoughtful decision.

LEARNING ACTIVITIES

Unlike the phonics and vocabulary chapters in which any of the learning activities is a good match for whatever you wish to help your child learn, the activities for comprehension are more narrowly focused. As a consequence, the first thing you will be told is the comprehension ability for which each activity is best suited. In this way you are assured that the learning prescription you choose fits your child's needs.

When I choose special reading material for my own children, and when we select passages for the disabled readers who come to the university reading clinic, I consider first whether or not the words in the materials are easy or hard. Passages with easy words—words your child can read confidently—are the best ones for developing comprehension. The idea is to free your child from the arduous task of word recognition so that he can put his full effort into understanding the meaning of the words in each sentence.

To improve comprehension, your child must put almost all of his conscious effort into thinking about what he is reading. When reading selections have a generous sprinkling of words your child doesn't know, most of his energy is spent figuring out the vocabulary. The effort your child puts into word recognition cannot be used for comprehension. As a result, your child may learn new vocabulary words without his comprehension ability improving much.

1. THE MAIN POINT

When it comes to activities for finding the main idea, the Main Point is my favorite and a favorite of classroom teachers, too. Aside from the fact that it is a great learning activity, this game can be modified to suit children of any age and reading level.

If your child is in the fourth grade or beyond, clip short articles from children's magazines or the newspaper. (The sports page is a good source of easier-to-read newspaper articles.) Write a number on the back of each article and its title. Then cut titles from articles and put them in an envelope for safekeeping. Now your child is ready to begin.

Ask your child to read each article and think of a title describing the main idea. Once your child has come up with a good title, ask him to write it on a strip of paper and clip it to the article. Next, have your child look at the titles you have cut from the articles and match the correct title with each article he has read. Since the titles and articles will have the same numbers on the back, you can double-check your child's choices. Now compare the title your child wrote and the title your child chose with the title the author used and talk about why some titles give the gist of an article better than others.

If matching titles with articles is too challenging for your child, matching articles and pictures is another, easier version. A third variation is to have your child draw a picture explaining the main point of an article. The idea behind these two adaptations is to use pictures as a bridge for understanding the main idea in a reading passage.

The three versions of the Main Point described thus far require that your child read well enough to understand articles from children's magazines or newspapers. If your child is too young for this kind of reading, or if your child does not read well enough, you can still use the Main Point. Begin by cutting out interesting pictures from magazines— choose pictures that show a good bit of action—and tape or paste each one to a blank sheet of paper.

Show your child pictures one at a time, asking "What do you think this picture is about?" Discuss the gist of the picture, and when your child has arrived at a good description of the main point, write it underneath like a caption. This is a terrific way to introduce the main idea and is an activity your younger child or less-skilled reader is bound to enjoy.

2. COLOR CUES

If your child needs some extra practice finding the main idea or locating facts and details, Color Cues is a superb activity. Over the years I have used this activity often. Color Cues comes at the top of my list because it is an excellent means of showing children the link between the main idea and its supporting facts and details. In reality, these two comprehension skills are blended when your child reads, yet many learning activities keep them separate. Not only does Color Cues help your child to see how these two abilities are interwoven, but it improves both at once!

You'll need short reading passages (articles from children's magazines are perfect for this activity) and two colored markers to do this activity—any light colors will do as long as the markers are transparent enough to allow print to show through. (Highlighters are great if you have them on hand.)

First, have your child read a short passage or an article and use a colored marker to highlight the main idea. Use a different colored marker to highlight supporting facts and details. Once finished, your child can look at highlighted areas and be able to tell you quickly about an article, as well as give you the facts and details.

3. TREASURE HUNT

Going on a treasure hunt is a wonderful way to help your child learn to follow directions. Hide a treasure—any treasure will do—and write step-by-step directions leading your child to the hiding place. Write each step on a separate piece of paper, putting the first on the kitchen cabinet (or some other prominent place). Hide the other steps in places your child can find only by following your directions in sequence.

If your child is a beginning reader or is having particular difficulty following directions, begin with simple directions having only one or two steps, like "Look under the sofa." When your child lifts up the pillow, there will be another clue saying, "Go to your bedroom and look inside your closet." Write multi-step directions for older, more advanced readers—"In the kitchen you'll find a clue at the back of the third drawer to the right of the sink." If your child can find treasures on hunts with directions like these, he is doing well!

4. WHAT'S MISSING?
Here is another activity aimed at helping your child to understand directions. Begin with a set of directions for something your child knows how to do well, and leave out one crucial step.

Chocolate pudding is one of my children's favorite desserts, so I wrote out a set of directions for making instant pudding like this: "First, get out a box of pudding. Pour the pudding in a bowl. Next, get out some milk. Use the mixer to beat up the pudding. Last, pour the pudding into small bowls and refrigerate." What's the missing step? Pouring the milk in the bowl is missing—no milk, no pudding. This game is somewhat like solving a riddle—your child will love it! What's more, it's a sound, successful teaching idea.

Here is another way to use What's Missing?: ask your child to write the directions. My daughter, who loves to make peanut-butter-and-jelly sandwiches, wrote this set of directions. "First get out a spoon and knife. Now get two pieces of bread. Take one piece of bread, get the peanut butter, open the peanut butter and spread it on one piece of bread. Now one side is done. Take the other piece of bread. Get a spoon and stick it in the jelly. Get a glob of jelly on the spoon. Pull the spoon out. Put the jelly on the other piece of bread and put the spoon down. Pick up the knife and spread the jelly. Put down the knife. Put the two pieces of bread together." What's missing? Well, I had to think about that one, but eventually I figured it out. Putting the knife down after spreading the peanut butter is the missing step.

Sometimes a long set of directions can be a bit over-whelming for younger children. If you sense that your child is discouraged by the thought of so much writing, ask him to dictate a set of directions that you can write for him. What's crucial is to get your child thinking about a logical sequence of steps and becoming aware of signal words like **first, second, next,** and **then.**

5. GET IT STRAIGHT

If your child likes to draw or act, this is a great activity for learning correct order. The idea behind Get It Straight is for your child to portray, either through drawing or pan-tomiming, the correct sequence of events in a story. If your child enjoys artwork, have him read a story and draw pic-tures that show each major happening, one after the other. Should your child be unable to read storybooks on his own, Get It Straight still makes a fine learning activity. Just ask your child to draw a sequence of pictures illustrating some-thing he is familiar with—like going swimming, flowers blooming in the spring, or making a jack-o'-lantern, as shown in the illustration on the next page.

If your child would rather act out a story than draw it, ask him to pantomime the events. Actors need an audience, so ask other family members to watch your child and guess what he is portraying. Pantomiming has the advantage of involving an active, supportive audience. Either way, with artwork or pantomime, your child's ability to detect correct order will get better and better.

6. COMIC LINEUP

Comic Lineup is a favorite of every child I know, suited to children of any age and highly entertaining. As the name implies, Comic Lineup uses comic strips to teach correct order. If your child is young, say a first- or beginning second-grader, cut out a comic strip with no more than three frames. If your child is older, use as many frames as you believe your child is capable of thinking about at one time.

Once you have found a good comic strip, cut it into separate frames and scramble them. Show your child the mixed-up frames and say, "Here is a comic strip with the parts all mixed up. See if you can put them in the correct order." If your child confuses the order of events, talk about what a logical order might look like and help your child to arrange the frames properly. As your child becomes skilled at this activity, use comic strips with more frames.

7. WHAT NEXT?

If your child needs extra practice determining cause and effect, What Next? is a good learning activity. To play What Next? your child must match cards that have causes written on them with cards that have effects.

Before playing the game, make a deck of twenty-four

cards—twelve cards with a cause written on each and twelve with effects. Write the causes in yellow ink on three-by-five cards and the effects in red. Once you have made a deck of cause-and-effect cards, shuffle it and deal six cards to each player. Put the rest of the cards facedown in a stack on the table and turn the first card faceup.

Each player takes turns trying to match a card in his hand with the card faceup on the table. Any reasonable "cause-and-effect" combination is permissible. If a player has a match or wants to bluff, he says "I can match 'X,' reading the cause or effect written on the faceup card." If the other players do not challenge him, he picks up the card, puts it with a card from his hand, and places both cards facedown on the table. Another card is turned faceup and the game continues. However, if another person wants to challenge, he says, "What next?" When challenged, a player must put both cards faceup on the table for all to see. If a feasible cause-and-effect combination exists, the player turns the cards facedown and the person who challenged him has to draw an extra card. But if the player was bluffing and the cause-effect combination isn't a reasonable one, the player must put both cards back in his hand and draw an additional card from the stack. The person who gets rid of all of his cards first wins the game.

8. SIGNAL

Signal is a homemade board game that is suitable for children of any age. As with Sound Race in Chapter 10, use an old board, if you have one, from a game your child no longer plays and modify it, or make one with tagboard or cardboard. On the board, draw a winding trail of rectangles beginning at the bottom with START and moving to FINISH at the top.

Next, make a stack of cards with cause-and-effect relationships telling players what to do. For example, a card might read, "**Because** you had a cold, you missed school and have to go back three squares." Or it could read, "**Since you got a hundred on your spelling test, move ahead six spaces.**" Be sure to use signal words (**because, if, due to, when, since, therefore, as a result of, as a consequence, unless, hence, in order that, for, so, so that, as,** and **then**) when you make cards.

To play, put the cards in a stack facedown. Take turns drawing cards and following instructions. This game gives your child lots of valuable practice reading and understanding cause-and-effect relationships. Because second-grade Eddie was a real fan of board games, his mother made the version of Signal shown in the drawing that follows. The game is easy enough for Eddie's five-year-old sister to play, which makes it extra fun!

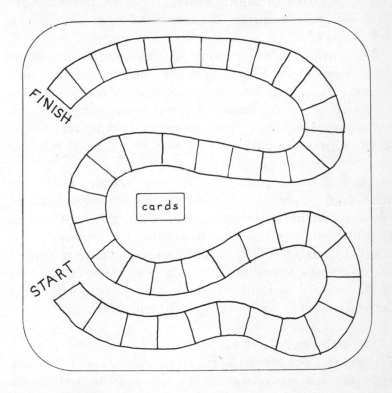

9. LOADED WORDS

One of the most powerful, persuasive tools at an author's disposal is the use of emotion-packed words. As an effective propaganda technique, the use of emotion-packed words is something older elementary-age children should understand. Loaded Words is a fun, easy, and effective way to help your fourth- through sixth-grader to recognize propaganda when emotion-packed words are used.

I prefer to use advertisements for this activity, but anything that makes liberal use of highly charged words is fine. When you have collected several ads, ask your child to read each one and circle the loaded words. Sometimes they stand alone, like **enchanting** and **charming.** Other times loaded words can be found in phrases and sentences—**crafted in high quality, imported porcelain,** or **professionally maintained gardens of exquisite beauty,** for example.

Sixth-grader Charlie found all these words in a single advertisement for a housing development: gracious townhouses; distinctive homes; all the finer things in life are free at _____ (name of the community); delightful shopping areas; superlative home crafted by one of the most respected builders; professionally planned community; secluded neighborhoods; etc.

Loaded Words is always a hit with fourth-, fifth-, and sixth-grade children. Not only is it challenging; it also teaches valuable lessons in critical reading that go beyond picking out emotion-packed words. By focusing your child's attention on how authors use emotion-packed words artfully, your child becomes more aware of attempts made to sway his thinking. As a consequence, your child becomes a better, more thoughtful consumer.

10. FRACTURED TALES

Fractured Tales sounds a bit like an activity for very young children, but, in reality, it calls for sophisticated critical reading abilities. Its aim is to improve your child's ability to detect a bias. This is accomplished by the retelling of familiar stories from the point of view of the characters who are villains or bystanders. For example, "The Three Little Pigs" might be told from the wolf's perspective, or "Little Miss Muffet" from the point of view of the spider.

Stories can be retold aloud or can be written on paper. But the important thing is *not* to name the character from whose point of view the story is being told. This way the reader (or listener) must detect the bias on his own. Once the reader (or listener) thinks he knows whose point of view is being expressed, he must give three reasons to support this claim. Either you or your child can do the retelling, whatever works best.

11. CAN YOU PROVE IT?

A challenging test of comprehension, knowing and identifying the difference between fact and opinion are abilities your fourth-, fifth-, or sixth-grader will need a great deal of practice to master. Can You Prove It? is an activity that uses newspaper and magazine articles to illustrate for your child the difference between fact and opinion.

Begin by selecting a few interesting articles from children's magazines or the newspaper. Look on the sports page or in life-style sections of the newspaper for easier articles. Use two colored markers—the kind that are transparent enough to let print show through—to highlight all of the facts in one color and the opinions in another.

Have your child read the sentences you've highlighted, asking "Can you prove it?" If your child knows where to find the information to prove a statement, the answer is "Yes"—the statement is a fact. If he cannot prove it, his "No" answer means that the statement is an opinion.

Once your child is skilled at differentiating between fact and opinion, ask him to do the highlighting. This changes the focus of the activity so that now *you* must answer the question "Can you prove it?" Regardless of who does the highlighting and who does the answering, it's great fun to count the number of facts and opinions used by authors. It gives your child an important insight into the way authors present information—information that your child will use in his everyday reading and that will go a long way toward making your child a good, critical reader.

13

LITERACY BEGINS
AT HOME

"I know that story," said four-year-old Jackson as he began turning the pages of John Vernon Lord and Janet Burroway's book *The Giant Jam Sandwich* (50). "I have it at home. My mom reads it. It's about a sandwich." Having read this humorous story about a wasp-plagued village to my own children, I believed that it might interest the four-year-olds in the day-care center that I was visiting.

As I glanced around the room I saw twenty children—some playing with blocks, others coloring, one group pretending to cook dinner with child-sized pots and pans. Next year the children would enter the elementary school reading program and begin to climb the reading pyramid. Years of experience show that children like Jackson, whose parents share reading experiences at home, are likely to become good readers. Children who enter kindergarten knowing that the words on the page—not the pictures—convey meaning, that pages are read from top to bottom, and who recognize a few words in the environment will probably be the best readers.

Without diminishing the contribution made by dedicated teachers, it should be recognized that parents are the single greatest influence on their children's future success in school. Where do children first learn about books? They learn at home—in a survey of 1,000 families, 47 percent of the mothers were credited with encouraging their children's interest in books and 14 percent of the fathers; in 16 percent of the families both parents encouraged reading (75). This same group considered reading to be the single most significant element in their children's formal education; 97 percent rated reading above all other subjects in its contribution to academic success, and 91 percent believed that reading was very important to their children's future.

Nationwide, we are spending over $300 billion per year to educate people of all ages. Reading has been a topic of national debate for nearly three decades—government, industry, and foundations have all spent large sums conducting surveys, assessing children's skills, and writing reports that outline the means to improve our nation's reading skills. Yet large numbers of individuals who seek employment do not have the necessary reading ability to pass entry-level examinations—one firm found that 84 percent of applicants from a major metropolitan area failed to qualify for employment when tested on skills related to vocabulary, number concepts, and problem-solving (76).

Perhaps equally alarming is the fact that standards for literacy are rising. It is predicted that jobs in the middle of the "skill range" today are likely to be the least-skilled jobs of tomorrow. By the year 2000, some level of postsecondary education will probably be necessary to hold the majority of jobs (77). This means that the workplace of the future may provide job opportunities only for high school graduates who have well-developed reading abilities. In order to remain competitive in the world marketplace, the number of high school graduates who are good readers will probably have to increase. Strengthening the home-school connection, then, may be the best means of improving children's reading achievement. Working cooperatively, parents and teachers may provide the kind of education programs that will result in literate, well-educated children.

Since the 1960s there has been an increasing emphasis on involving parents in their children's elementary school education. A high priority in many schools, "Parent Involvement" is an accepted component of the elementary school reading program. For example, schools that receive federal funds under Chapter I—a national program to improve the reading and math skills of underachieving, disadvantaged children—are required by law to involve parents in their children's education. The current emphasis on parent involvement contrasts sharply with the beliefs held by educators several decades ago when the prevailing view was that parents should *not* attempt to help their children to read at home. The thinking at that time was that the school should have full responsibility for teaching children to read, and parental involvement was not advocated. Today most teachers encourage parents to join with the elementary school and share the responsibility for their children's learning.

When I think about the powerful influence that parents *can* have on their children's lives, I recall the contribution made by the father of six-year-old Ralph. As a preschooler and kindergartner, Ralph was a bright-eyed, eager youngster. His parents read aloud to him frequently, and he was interested in books and looked forward to beginning the first grade. Upon entering the first grade, Ralph knew the names of the letters of the alphabet, how to write his name, and how to read a few words. From all indications, Ralph should have gotten off to a terrific start as a first-grader.

Soon after the start of the new school year, however,

Ralph appeared to lose interest in school. He said that he didn't want to go to the first grade, complained of stomachaches, and, for the first time, seemed to lose interest in books. Ralph's parents were puzzled. In February, his teacher told Ralph's parents that he was unable to read the easiest first-grade book. Recognizing that Ralph was having difficulty, his father came to me for advice. I lent him a great number of easy-to-read books and suggested that he read with Ralph for fifteen minutes every evening. Four months later Ralph's father returned the books. "How is Ralph doing?" I asked. "Terrific" was his reply. "Ralph is reading as well as the other children in his class. He loves school!"

Ralph's father accepted the responsibility for a portion of his son's progress in reading and worked cooperatively with Ralph's first-grade teacher in support of the elementary school reading program. Still, I was curious about the reason for Ralph's indifference to reading during the first half of the year. The story Ralph's father told was interesting. Having a great deal of enthusiasm for learning to read, Ralph expected that he would become a reader within the first few weeks of school. When October rolled around and Ralph was not reading as well as his older siblings, he assumed that he would never learn, and stopped trying. Reading the easy-to-read books demonstrated to Ralph that he *could* learn—his negative self-image started to change. Gradually he began to feel confident and to perceive himself as a successful reader. His improved self-concept had a positive effect on his reading achievement—as a second-grader, Ralph was among the best readers in his class. Years later, I talked to Ralph; he told me that he had graduated at the top of his high school class and received a full scholarship to attend a fine university.

My oldest child is close to the age Ralph was when we first met. As a parent, my aim is to provide the support that is necessary for my children to make steady progress climbing the reading pyramid. In order to do this, I spend a minimum of fifteen minutes after dinner with my daughter while she reads library books. Fifteen minutes is a goal that can be attained easily—some nights we spend much longer—and the benefits of regular practice reading are tremendous. We also use the phonics, vocabulary, and comprehension activities explained in Chapters 10, 11, and 12 to reinforce the reading abilities that Susan is learning in her classroom. Our family routinely enjoys read-aloud books, and we visit the public library regularly.

I have found that locating books well-suited to the interests and abilities of children has a profound effect on their eagerness to read for pleasure. If your child, like mine, occasionally requires some guidance in selecting interesting and appropriate books, refer to the suggestions in Chapter 2, Matching Children with Books, and use the books that I have listed in the Notes as a resource. (Books in the Notes are only a sample of the many wonderful books that are written for children.) You may want to ask the librarian in the youth section of your public library to recommend books that are similar in topic or reading level to those listed in the Notes. If you live in a large city, visit a bookstore for children—one that sells children's books exclusively—where you are likely to find well-informed employees and an extensive selection from which to choose. If there are no bookstores exclusively for children near your home, look for one when you travel—it will likely be worth the extra effort that it takes to find one!

Years of experience have shown that when the principles set out in this book are followed, the chances are high that children will become good readers. Set aside time during the day for your child to read—ask that he turn off the television and radio, and concentrate on reading. Read aloud to your child—read frequently and from a variety of books. Make books and other reading materials readily available in your home, and share with your child some of the things that you are reading or have read. Newspaper and magazine articles, pamphlets, brochures, and novels make interesting topics of conversation, and you will send a clear message to your child that you value reading by discussing them.

Work to support your elementary school's reading program—use the activities in this book to help your child at home with phonics, vocabulary, and comprehension; pay close attention to the books and papers your child brings home from school; talk frequently with your child's teacher. As a result, your child will most probably become a better reader and develop a lifelong habit of reading for pleasure. Your child's life—and your life, too—will be enriched by the many wonderful books written for young readers and by sharing books at home. And perhaps more important, you will be transmitting the perception that reading—reading often and reading well—is a high priority and is crucial for living successfully in a complex, high-tech society.

NOTES

BOOKS FOR CHILDREN

1. Sharmat, M. W. A series of books featuring Nate the Great, available in paperback from Dell Publishing Company, New York. Included among the titles in this series are: *Nate the Great; Nate the Great and the Fishy Prize; Nate the Great and the Phony Clue;* and *Nate the Great and the Snowy Trail.*

2. Parish, P. A series of books featuring Amelia Bedelia. Included among the titles in this series, available in paperback from Avon Books, New York, are: *Amelia Bedelia Goes Camping; Amelia Bedelia and the Baby; Amelia Bedelia Helps Out;* and *Good Work, Amelia Bedelia.*

3. Lobel, A. A series of books featuring Frog and Toad, available in paperback from Harper & Row, New York. Included among the titles in the series are: *Frog and Toad; Days with Frog and Toad; Frog and Toad All Year; Frog and Toad Are Friends;* and *Frog and Toad Together.*

4. Sobol, D. A series of books featuring Encyclopedia Brown, available in paperback from Scholastic Inc., Bantam Books, or Dell Publishing Company, Inc., all located in New York.

Included among the titles in this extensive series are: *Encyclopedia Brown, Boy Detective; Encyclopedia Brown and the Case of the Secret Pitch; Encyclopedia Brown Saves the Day;* and *Encyclopedia Brown Takes the Case.*

5. Fitzgerald, J. D. A series of books featuring the Great Brain, available in paperback from Dell Publishing Company, New York. Included among the many titles in this series are: *The Great Brain; The Great Brain at the Academy; The Great Brain Reforms;* and *The Return of the Great Brain.*

6. Cleary, B. Books featuring Henry Huggins, and Ramona; most titles in these series are available in paperback from Dell Publishing Company, New York. Included among the titles are: *Henry and Beezus; Henry and the Clubhouse; Henry and Ribsy; Henry and the Paper Route; Ramona the Pest; Ramona and Her Friends; Ramona and Her Father; Ramona Quimby, Age Eight;* and *Ramona the Brave.*

7. Farley, W. A series of books featuring the Black Stallion, available in paperback from Random House, New York. Included among the titles in this extensive series are: *The Black Stallion and Flame; The Black Stallion Challenged; The Black Stallion's Courage;* and *The Black Stallion Mystery.*

8. Henry, M. A series of horse stories available in paperback from Macmillan, New York. Included among the titles in this extensive series are: *Born to Trot; King of the Wind; Mustang, Wild Spirit of the West;* and *White Stallion of Lipizza.*

9. Naylor, P. R. A series of witch stories available in paperback from Dell Publishing Company, Inc., New York. Included among the titles in this series are: *The Witch Herself; Witch's Sister;* and *Witch Water.*

10. Alexander, L. *The Prydain Chronicles.* A series of books available in paperback from Dell Publishing Company, Inc., New York. Included among the titles in this series are: *The Book of Three; The High King;* and *The Black Cauldron.*

11. Cooper, S. *The Dark Is Rising.* The first book in this series, *Over Sea, Under Stone,* is available in paperback from Harcourt Brace Jovanovich, San Diego. The other titles in this

series—*The Dark Is Rising; Greenwitch; The Grey King;* and *Silver on the Tree*—are available in paperback from Macmillan, New York.

12. L'Engle, M. *A Wrinkle in Time; A Wind in the Door; A Swiftly Tilting Planet.* A series of books available in paperback from Dell Publishing Company, Inc., New York.

13. Marshall, E. G. (1984). *Fox All Week.* New York: Dial Books for Young Readers. Other books written by this author and available from the same publisher include: *Fox and His Friends; Fox in Love; Fox on Wheels; Fox at School; Four on the Shore; Three by the Sea; Troll Country.*

14. Christian, M. B. (1983). *Swamp Monsters.* New York: Dial Books for Young Readers.

15. *Dial Easy-to-Read Books.* A series of books written for young readers, available in paperback from Dial Books for Young Readers, New York. Included among the many titles are: *Molly Moves Out,* written by Susan Pearson; *The Dog Food Caper* and *The Poison Ivy Case,* written by Joan M. Lexau; and *Blue Sun Ben, Red Sun Girl* and *Ruthie's Rude Friends,* written by Jean and Claudio Marzollo.

16. Minarik, E. H. A series of books featuring Little Bear, available in paperback from Harper & Row, New York. Included among the titles in this series are: *Little Bear's Visit; Father Bear Comes Home;* and *Little Bear.*

17. Ziefert, H. *Hello Reading!* This series is available in paperback from Puffin Books, New York, and includes multiple titles.

18. *STEP into Reading.* A series of books for young readers available in paperback from Random House, New York.

19. Ziefert, H. A series of books featuring the children who belong to the Small Potatoes Club, available in paperback from Dell Publishing Company, New York. Included among the titles in this series are: *The Small Potatoes Club; The Small Potatoes' Busy Beach Day;* and *The Small Potatoes and the Snowball Fight.* Books coauthored with Jon Ziefert include: *The*

Small Potatoes and the Magic Show; The Small Potatoes and the Birthday Party; and *The Small Potatoes and the Sleep-Over.*

20. Giff, P. R. A series of books featuring the Kids of the Polk Street School, available in paperback from Dell Publishing Company, Inc., New York. Included among the many titles in this series are: *The Beast in Ms. Rooney's Room; In the Dinosaur's Paw;* and *Fish Face.*

21. Adler, D. A. A series of books featuring Cam Jansen, available in paperback from Dell Publishing Company, New York. Included among the titles in this series are: *Cam Jansen and the Mystery of the Gold Coins; Cam Jansen and the Mystery of the U.F.O.; Cam Jansen and the Mystery of the Television Dog;* and *Cam Jansen and the Mystery of the Dinosaur Bones.*

22. Adler, D. A. A series of books featuring twins, available in paperback from Penguin Books, New York. Included among the titles in this series are: *The Fourth Floor Twins and the Disappearing Parrot Trick; The Fourth Floor Twins and the Fish Snitch Mystery; The Fourth Floor Twins and the Fortune Cookie;* and *The Fourth Floor Twins and the Silver Ghost.*

23. Lindgren, A. (1988). *Pippi Longstocking.* New York: Puffin Books. Also look for *Pippi Goes on Board* and *Pippi in the South Seas,* written by the same author and available from the same publisher.

24. MacDonald, B. A series of books featuring Mrs. Piggle-Wiggle, available in paperback from Harper & Row, New York. Included among the titles in this series are: *Hello, Mrs. Piggle-Wiggle,* originally copyrighted in 1957 and published as a First Harper Trophy edition in 1985; *Mrs. Piggle-Wiggle; Mrs. Piggle-Wiggle's Magic;* and *Mrs. Piggle-Wiggle's Farm.*

25. Howe, J. Books written by James Howe include: *The Celery Stalks at Midnight; Howliday Inn; A Night Without Stars;* and *Morgan's Zoo,* available in paperback from Avon Books, New York.

26. Howe, D., and J. Howe (1979). *Bunnicula: A Rabbit-Tale of Mystery.* New York: Avon Books.

27. Gilson, J. (1988). *Hobie Hanson, You're Weird.* New York:

Pocket Books. Also look for *13 Ways to Sink a Sub* and *4B Goes Wild,* written by the same author and available from Archway Paperbacks.

28. Christopher, M. (1981). *Tight End.* Boston, Mass.: Little, Brown and Company. Examples of other titles by the same author are: *Look Who's Playing First Base; Catcher with a Glass Arm; Dirt Bike Racer;* and *Ice Magic.*

29. *The American Girls Collection.* There are nine titles in this series of books: three books focus on the life of Kirsten in 1854, three on Samantha in 1904, and three on Molly in 1944. All titles are available in paperback from the Pleasant Company, Madison, Wisconsin.

30. MacLachlan, P. (1985). *Sarah, Plain and Tall.* New York: Harper & Row. Also look for *Cassie Binegar; Through Grandpa's Eyes;* and *Unclaimed Treasures,* written by the same author and available from the same publisher.

31. Blume, J. (1980). *Superfudge.* New York: Dell Publishing Company. Examples of other titles by the same author are: *Are You There God? It's Me, Margaret; Tales of a Fourth-Grade Nothing; Otherwise Known as Sheila the Great;* and *Blubber.*

32. Roberts, W. D. (1975). *The View from the Cherry Tree.* New York: Macmillan.

33. Bellairs, J. Included among the books written by John Bellairs are: *The House with a Clock in Its Walls; The Figure in the Shadows; The Letter, the Witch, and the Ring; The Mummy, the Will and the Crypt;* and *The Curse of the Blue Figurine,* available in paperback from Bantam Books, New York.

34. Snyder, Z. K. Included among the books written by Zilpha Keatley Snyder are: *The Egypt Game; The Headless Cupid; Blair's Nightmare;* and *The Famous Stanley Kidnapping Case,* available in paperback from Dell Publishing Company, Inc., New York.

35. Kjelgaard, J. (1945). *Big Red.* New York: Bantam Books. Also look for: *Desert Dog; Stormy; Snow Dog; Lion Hound; Outlaw Red; Haunt Fox; Irish Red: Son of Big Red; A Nose for*

Trouble; and *Wild Trek,* available in paperback from Bantam Books, New York.

36. Ward, L. (1952). *The Biggest Bear.* Boston, Mass.: Houghton Mifflin Company.

37. Keats, E. J. (1962). *The Snowy Day.* New York: Viking Press.

38. Dahl, R. (1961). *James and the Giant Peach.* New York: Bantam Books. Other books written by this author include: *Charlie and the Chocolate Factory; Charlie and the Great Glass Elevator; Danny the Champion of the World;* and *Fantastic Mr. Fox.*

39. Byars, B. (1982). *The Two-Thousand-Pound Goldfish.* New York: Scholastic Inc.

40. Bare, C. S. (1986). *To Love a Cat.* New York: Dodd, Mead and Company.

41. de Brunhoff, J. (1963). *Babar the King.* New York: Random House. Included among the titles in this extensive series are: *Babar and the Ghost; Babar and the Professor; Babar's Birthday Surprise;* and *Babar's Mystery,* available from Random House.

42. Rockwell, T. (1973). *How to Eat Fried Worms.* New York: Dell Publishing Co. Other books written by this author include: *Rackety-Bang and Other Verses; Humph!; The Neon Motorcycle;* and *Squawwwk!,* available in paperback from the same publisher.

43. Cole, J. (1983). *Bony-Legs.* New York: Scholastic Inc.

44. Collier, E. (1956). *The Story of Annie Oakley.* New York: Grosset & Dunlap.

45. Lewis, C. S. (1951). *Prince Caspian.* New York: Macmillan. The titles in this series, which is called *The Chronicles of Narnia,* are: *The Lion, the Witch and the Wardrobe; Prince Caspian; The Voyage of the "Dawn Treader"; The Silver Chair; The Horse and His Boy; The Magician's Nephew;* and *The Last Battle.*

46. Erickson, R. E. (1974). *A Toad for Tuesday.* New York: Lothrop, Lee & Shepard Co.

47. Sendak, M. (1963). *Where the Wild Things Are.* New York:

Harper & Row. If your child enjoys this book, look for *In the Night Kitchen* (1970), written by the same author and available from the same publisher.

48. Sendak, M. (1975). *Really Rosie.* New York: Harper & Row.

49. Howe, J. (1984). *Morgan's Zoo.* New York: Avon Books.

50. Lord, J. V., and J. Burroway (1972). *The Giant Jam Sandwich.* Boston, Mass.: Houghton Mifflin Company.

RESOURCES FOR PARENTS

51. Write the International Reading Association at P.O. Box 8139, 800 Barksdale Road, Newark, N.J. 19714-8139 to obtain a copy of the most recent Children's Choices list. Include a self-addressed envelope with first-class postage for four ounces.

52. Kobrin, B. (1988). *Eyeopeners! How to Choose and Use Children's Books About Real People, Places, and Things.* New York: Viking/ Penguin Inc.

53. Trelease, J. (1985). *The Read-Aloud Handbook.* New York: Penguin Books.

54. Fry, E. (1977). "Fry's Readability Graph: Clarifications, Validity, and Extension to Level 17." *Journal of Reading,* 21, pp. 242–52.

55. Write to the Children's Book Council at 67 Irving Place, New York, N.Y. 10003, to get information on children's paperback book clubs.

56. *The Dolch Basic Sight Vocabulary,* authored by E. W. Dolch, is available on cards from Garrard Publishing Company, Champaign, Illinois 61820.

REFERENCES

57. Manzo, A. V. (1969). "The ReQuest Procedure." *Journal of Reading,* 13, pp. 123–26.

58. Gitelman, H. F., and S. R. Rasberry (1986). "Bring on the Books: A Schoolwide Contest." *The Reading Teacher,* 39, pp. 905–7.

59. Ekwall, E. E., and J. L. Shanker (1985). *Teaching Reading in the Elementary School*. Columbus: Charles E. Merrill Publishing Co.

60. Anderson, R. C., E. H. Hiebert, J. A. Scott, and I. A. G. Wilkinson (1985). *Becoming a Nation of Readers*. Washington, D.C.: U.S. Department of Education.

61. Fielding, L. G., P. T. Wilson, and R. C. Anderson (1987). "A New Focus on Free Reading: The Role of Trade Books in Reading Instruction." In T. E. Raphael, ed., *Contexts of School-Based Literacy*. New York: Random House.

62. National Assessment of Educational Progress (1985). *The Reading Report Card: Progress Toward Excellence in Our Schools*. Princeton, N.J.: Educational Testing Service, Report No. 15-R-01.

63. Rossman, A. D. (1987). "Reading Automaticity: The Essential Element of Academic Success." *Principal*, 67, pp. 28–32.

64. Durkin, D. (1987). *Teaching Young Children to Read,* Fourth Edition. Boston, Mass.: Allyn and Bacon, Inc., p. 115.

65. Lovelace, T. (1980). "Enhancing the Lives of Nursing Home Patients Through Reading Activities." In L. S. Johnson, ed., *Reading and the Adult Learner*. Newark, Del.: International Reading Association.

66. Collins, J. (1982). "Discourse Style, Classroom Interaction and Differential Treatment." *Journal of Reading Behavior*, 14, pp. 429–37.

67. Bennett, W. J. (1987). *James Madison High School: A Curriculum for American Students*. Washington, D.C.: United States Department of Education.

68. *School Dropouts: The Extent and Nature of the Problem*. Briefing Report to Congressional Requesters. Washington, D.C.: Government Printing Office, 1986.

69. Lapointe, Archie. "The State of Instruction in Reading and Writing in U.S. Elementary Schools." *Phi Delta Kappan*, 68 (2), pp. 135–38, 1986.

70. Boder, E. (1971). "Developmental Dyslexia: Prevailing Diagnostic Concepts and a New Diagnostic Approach." In H. R. Myklebust, ed., *Progress in Learning Disabilities,* Vol. 2. New York: Gruen & Stratton, pp. 293–321.

71. Feingold, B. (1975). *Why Your Child Is Hyperactive.* New York: Random House.

72. Bennett, W. J. (1986). *First Lessons.* Washington, D.C.: U.S. Department of Education.

73. Mangieri, John N. (1978). "Dolch List Revisited." *Reading World,* 18 (1), 1978, pp. 91–95.

74. Fry, E. (1980). "The New Instant Word List." *The Reading Teacher,* 34, pp. 284–89. Fry's list can be found in the following: Miller, J. W., and M. McKenna (1989). *Teaching Reading in the Elementary Classroom.* Scottsdale, Ariz.: Gorsuch, Scarisbrick, Publishers; and Rupley, W. H., and T. R. Blair (1989). *Reading Diagnoses and Remediation, Third Edition.* Columbus, Ohio: Merrill Publishing Company.

75. *The Jell-O Desserts Family Reading Survey.* Conducted in cooperation with Reading Is Fundamental, Inc., by the Roper Organization, Inc., May 1988.

76. *The Bottom Line: Basic Skills in the Workplace.* A joint publication of the United States Department of Education, William J. Bennett, Secretary, and the United States Department of Labor, Ann McLaughlin, Secretary, 1988.

77. *WORKFORCE 2000: Work and Workers for the 21st Century.* Indianapolis: Hudson Institute, 1987.

INDEX